THE WAY OF RIGHTEOUSNESS

Licensed to Succeed

By Olutayo Robert-Ojajuni

FriesenPress

One Printers Way
Altona, MB R0G 0B0
Canada

www.friesenpress.com

Copyright © 2024 by Olutayo Robert-Ojajuni
First Edition — 2024

Foreword by Dr. Myles Munroe
Foreword by Pastor Matthew Ashimolowo

All rights reserved.

No part of this publication may be reproduced in any form, or by any means, electronic or mechanical, including photocopying, recording, or any information browsing, storage, or retrieval system, without permission in writing from FriesenPress.

ISBN
978-1-03-830098-0 (Hardcover)
978-1-03-830097-3 (Paperback)
978-1-03-830099-7 (eBook)

1. RELIGION, CHRISTIAN LIVING, PERSONAL GROWTH

Distributed to the trade by The Ingram Book Company

FOREWORD

Dr. Myles E. Munroe

Everybody wants to succeed! The pursuit for success is inherent in the human spirit. It is the most common motivation in the human race and yet only a few understand and ever achieve it.

This erudite, eloquent, and immensely thought-provoking work gets to the heart of the deepest passions and aspirations of the human heart- to discover the path to personal Success. Every human wants to experience success in life!

This is an indispensable reading for anyone who wants to understand his or her own potential for achieving greatness and to live life above the norm. This is a profound authoritative work that spans the wisdom of the ages and yet breaks new ground in its approach and will possibly become a classic in this and the next generation.

This exceptional work by Tayo Ojajuni is one of the most profound, practical, principle-centered approaches to this subject I have read in a long time. The author's approach to this timely issue brings a fresh breath of air that captivates the heart, engages the mind and inspires the spirit of the reader.

The author's ability to leap over complicated theological and metaphysical jargon and reduce complex theories to simple practical principles that the least among us can understand is amazing.

Licensed to Succeed will challenge the intellectual while embracing the laymen as it dismantles the mysteries of the soul search of mankind and delivers the profound in simplicity.

In *Licensed to Succeed*, Tayo's approach awakens in the reader the untapped inhibiters that retard our personal development and his antidotes empower us to rise above these self-defeating, self-limiting factors to a life of exploits in spiritual and mental advancement.

The author also integrates into each chapter the time-tested precepts giving each principle a practical application to life making the entire process people-friendly.

Every sentence of this book is pregnant with wisdom and I enjoyed the mind-expanding experience of this exciting book. I admonish you to plunge into this ocean of knowledge and watch your life change for the better as you discover that you are *Licensed to Succeed*.

FOREWORD

by Matthew Ashimolowo

The desire to succeed has been with man from time immemorial. Every endeavor people pursue is approached with success in mind. This cannot be coincidental; it must be because it is in the DNA of man, just as it is in our nature to crave for food.

This argument is premised upon the fact that the first words God spoke to man convey the command to be fruitful, multiply, replenish, subdue and have dominion.

Man's original mandate was to rulership—to be the king of the earth. After all, His word says "the earth he gave to the sons of men."

The totality of what man was licensed to become is encapsulated in the five words Fruitful, multiply, replenish, subdue and dominion. Each was a graduation from the other.

Fruitfulness is productivity—"Pro and Duct." Creating the duct for the flow of ideas, concepts, breakthroughs and abundance. Multiplication is for bringing increase to the productivity.

Replenishing is the filling of empty places with what has been produced. Adding new stock by supplying.

When you subdue, your product has exceeded the immediate territories and subjugated the lands beyond. This subduing could be economic, spiritual or mental.

Dominion is the divine authorization man has from God to exercise mastership over situations and circumstances Dominion gives you clout, say-so power or the upper hand.

From the day of creation, we were licensed to do these things.

Pastor Tayo Ojajuni has adequately, competently and robustly shown this ageless truth as the reason why those who know it rule and those who don't struggle.

This powerful book has tremendous content and would bring transformation to the reader's cerebral and spiritual life.

DEDICATION

I dedicate this book to my Strength and Shield, the Glory and the Lifter up of my head, Jesus Christ. Thank you for saving me.

To my lovely wife, Oluwabunmi-mi, more love and more wins together.

To our wonderful children, Tobi, Mowa, Timi and Mofe + Moye. You are the best and I love you.

ACKNOWLEDGEMENTS

Sincere appreciation goes to my father and mother in the Lord—Pastor and Pastor Mrs. E. A. Adeboye for their spiritual upbringing. It is indeed a privilege to be connected to you through Jesus Christ.

To a notable mentor—Bishop David Oyedepo, thanks for all that you do. The late Dr. Myles Munroe I say thank you for your foreword—you did this as far back as August 16th, 2012. God indeed work in ways we cannot understand. Your memory will forever be cherished.

I cannot thank Pastor Matthew Ashimolowo enough. Since 2012 you looked at the manuscript and advised on the steps to take to make the book God's masterpiece.

To the initiator of this work—Pastor Austin Ayeni, I say thank you. After a teaching on this topic, you came to me and said, "you need to write a book from this." I am sure that you don't even remember.

To my parents, siblings and in-laws, I doff my hat for you. I appreciate the candid observations and diligence of Enwongo and ID.

To all the ministers and members of RCCG—The King's Covenant, Toronto Canada, you are indeed co-laborers in the Lord. It is great to be part of this heaven bound family.

To all those who worked on this book at Friesen press my appreciation is profound.

To all Kingdom Citizens, be rest assured that when you choose the way of righteousness, you are licensed to succeed.

CONTENTS

Foreword iii

Foreword v

Dedication vii

Acknowledgements ix

Introduction xiii

1. The License 1
2. Your DNA 13
3. Flourish 45
4. Evolve 61
5. The Components 101
6. The Know How 117
7. Don't Squint 129
8. 20/20 135

Praise For *Licensed To Succeed* 139

About the Author 143

INTRODUCTION

A timeless, barrier-breaking, prejudice-overcoming, tenet-tearing, and creed-crushing pronouncement that has worked in the favor of every man or woman no matter his or her leaning is the statement "Let us make man in our image after our likeness" (Gen. 1:26, KJV)

This statement, despite the fact that some people may have a religious knowledge of it, countless others are ignorant of it and its efficacious power to propel people in the direction of stardom and a success-filled life, but it is still potent in its ability to burgeon the discerning.

As if the first statement was not enough to thrust any person to live a success-driven life, then another word came: "… have dominion" (Gen. 1:28, KJV)

These two pronouncements have and are still shaping the course of mankind till today. Due to the fact that the mandate for dominion was given to mankind, it means all mankind, whether wicked or saint, has the capacity to make a success of their lives (depending on each person's definition of success) on this terra firma.

The statements reveal the mind of God for mankind at the onset of creation. It shows that the intention of divinity for humanity is victorious living, and this is still true today. The Almighty God spoke those words into the life of humanity not yet formed due to the extent of his love. His love is unparallel, impartial, wider than the ocean, broader than the heavens, higher than the skies, and extends even to the hopeless.

Even though man has done everything to make him withdraw this privilege, he has remained true to his word. He is the truth, and he cannot lie. His word spoken must accomplish the purpose for which it has been sent. He has not taken back this word that is filled with blessings. The caveat to the statement is that it now has as a partner: labor.

> All your life you will struggle to scratch a living from the ground…All your life you will sweat to produce food. (Gen. 3:17–18, NLT)

What this means is that any man who is able to put in a measure of labor, whether cerebral or visceral, is able to attain success or move from the troughs of life to exhilarating peaks based on the individual's pedestal. But all the success that such a person would have attained is just here on this earth. This kind of success does not transcend this cosmos, and it also has both the latent and kinetic capacity to be filled with sorrow at any moment because it does not have the active backing of the Almighty.

Whether in the rugged mountains of Tora Bora in Afghanistan; the prairie of Pampas of Argentina; the steppes of Eurasia; the igloo of Iqaluit, Nunavut; the sere desert of the Sahara; the peaks of the Himalayas; the swamp of the Sudd and the Okavango Delta; or the monsoon of Vietnam, every man—irrespective of location, faith, or creed—has the chance to succeed.

You may be Hispanic or Caucasian, colored or not colored, Aryan or Indian, Jew or Arab; the creative statement and its attendant blessing to be in dominion has given everyone the opportunity, whether male or female, the chance to be successful.

It is based on this that you see in real life the "non-Christians" doing well. They are hovering under the umbrella of "…have dominion," spoken by a loving God. This alone should make the so-called unbelievers in the Only Wise God shudder in trepidation regarding the awesomeness, wisdom, and compassion of God.

As man begins to enjoy relative success, the necessity for God—the conduit and creator of the success—becomes irrelevant. Those who have such belief fail to realize that there will be accountability for the life lived here on earth. "What does it profit a man if he gains this whole world and then loses his soul?"

When you now begin to understand that success transcends the earthly to the eternal, you realize there are definitely different levels of success. Enduring and good success is that which goes beyond your accomplishment on earth while also ensuring peace as a security while on earth and, furthermore, gives you access into the abode of God, paving the way for him to welcome you with warm accolades.

God the Almighty himself had to draw a distinction between success(es) when he advised a man by the name Joshua to be bold, to read, and to meditate on the Word of God so as to make his way prosperous to pave the way for "good success."

This pronouncement has become a curveball that many are not ready to deal with. This has raised the bar or shifted the expectation on what success is. It definitely means that some success(es) can be bad, if there is good success.

Even though every man has been designed for a success-driven life based on God's pronouncements on man—to be fruitful and multiply, and take dominion, (all a temporary permit for success)—this can be short-lived when a recipient flouts the privileges. It then becomes a snare and can be fraught with sorrows instead of prosperity, joy, and happiness.

Due to the new expectation for success—good success, for that matter, set by the Almighty God—a new way to be licensed for success had to be re-enacted, not just a temporary permit. You have to declare your intention to have it, and he will be the instructor who will approve your candidature after taking you through the necessary "road tests."

This license, when presented, causes everything and everyone to give you access. It is the Way of Righteousness--License to Succeed. While the previous permit, though general, ephemeral and earthly, comes with labor, this license based on free will intention only comes with work that produces result laced with favor. While the permit is labor filled, this license is grace filled wrapped up in righteousness.

The God of Excellence

> "The question is not whether the system works, but whether we like the way it works. Just because something works doesn't mean it is desirable. Concentration camps work, if your purpose is to enslave people. Stealing works, if all you care about is money. Lying works, if you don't give a damn about your personal integrity. Literally anything, no matter how monstrously immoral will work, depending on your desires and how you define the term work". (Sy Leon)

An irrefutable fact about God is that he is a righteous and excellent God. Anything short of excellence to him is an aberration. The book of James in the Bible gave a narration about him by saying, "Every good and perfect gift comes down from the Father of lights."

Righteousness per excellence projects him as dwelling in a light that is unapproachable. In His pursuit of excellence, he regularly reminds his children not to taint, tarnish, or forsake righteousness.

"When Abram was 99 years old, the Lord appeared to him. He said to Abram, 'I am God Almighty. Live in my presence with integrity'" (Gen. 17:1, GWT).

At this time, you would expect God to have been satisfied with the life of Abraham, but even with Abraham at ninety-nine years old, God was still saying, "I am a jealous God". He is jealous about the success he has deposited in you. He guards it lovingly, affectionately, and protectively.

For you to be able to live a life of fulfillment, you have to thirst daily for righteousness filled with excellence. Your being a special selection of God does not mean he will demand any less from you.

God met a man by the name Moses at the back side of the desert and told him he will be a deliverer. This was a statement that will make any man giddy with excitement, but the euphoria almost turned to ashes when God appeared to Moses again and the unexpected almost happened:

> "Along the way they stopped for the night. The Lord met Moses and tried to kill him. Then Zipporah took a flint knife, cut off her son's foreskin, and touched Moses feet with it. She said, "You are a bridegroom of blood to me." So the Lord let him alone." (Exod. 4:24–26, GWT)

Though God will not compromise excellence, but he cares about how the objective is met. Moses was focused on the message, but he was not really concerned about the pursuit. Everything you do has to be excellently done with righteousness—in your homes and in your relationship with your wife and children. If it cannot be well done with integrity, it is not worth doing.

Why Righteous Excellence?

Disorderliness distracts while orderliness attracts. The opposite of orderliness is mediocrity. God brought out the Israelites from Egypt in organized family groups despite the urgency to depart: "I will bring my people, the Israelites, out of Egypt in organized family groups" (Exod. 7:4b, GWT).

"If you don't have the time to do it right, where do you think you're going to find the time to do it over?" (Anonymous).

The psalmist said, "Unless the Lord builds the house, the work of the builders is wasted."

"Then Moses inspected all their work. When he found it had been done just as the Lord had commanded him, he blessed them" (Exod. 39:43, NLT).

It was only after Moses inspected the work that he pronounced blessings. When you consider that the craftsmen, architects, contractors, laborers, volunteers, and even donors would have spent countless man-hours in the building of the Ark, then you begin to understand the depth of the verse. Assuming they completed the work without following instructions, it would have been an exercise in futility.

This means if you are doing anything and it is not according to heavenly pattern, it is a wasted effort. Look at the category of people whom he inspected their work:

> "Moses called Bezalel and Oholiab and every other craftsman to whom the Lord had given these skills and who was willing to come and do the work." (Exod. 36:2, GWT)

These are people whom God had given divine wisdom. A thought that should permeate your being right now is, when your work is inspected, will it pass the test of excellence according to the standards of God?

> Every job is a self-portrait of the person who did it. Therefore, autograph your work with excellence. (Anonymous)

Are you following Godly instructions in all that you do? The question could be, What instructions? I will say, "wait a minute and consider wisely." The word of God says,

"Live in me, and I will live in you. A branch cannot produce any fruit by itself. It has to stay attached to the vine. In the same way you cannot produce fruit unless you live in me. I am the Vine. You are the branches. Those who live in me while I live in them will produce a lot of fruit. But you can't produce anything without me. Whoever doesn't live in me is thrown away like a branch and dries up. Branches like this are gathered, thrown into a fire, and burned." (John 15:4–6, GWT)

This definitely means that any measure of success that any individual has outside of him will eventually lead to being "thrown away like a branch and dries up. Branches like this are gathered, thrown into a fire, and burned."

Work your way up or rust your way out. (Holton)

Righteous Excellence brings about divine and human advertisement. Everybody wants to go from grass to grace and glory to glory. Nobody wants to go from grace to grass or honor to dishonor. This means that righteous excellence promotes. You have a duty to also promote excellence in everything that you do.

The only way to do this is if the God of excellence is in you. The success of righteous excellence is found in the solitude of integrity laced preparation. For you to truly function excellently, you need to follow the pattern of the excellent God. Here is the excellent way from the excellent God.

1

The License

Long before the first pronouncement came from the mouth of God saying, "Let there be light," He had already decided and preordained that he will create a people who will look like him. This people will be whole and holy.

He had it all planned out that you will be able to function in the highest heaven and on planet Earth. You will be abundantly free, and he will lavish you with gifts to enable you succeed in life. The good news today is that God has it all designed.

This is a classic case of the scale being skewed in your favor. The dice has been loaded, whether heads or tail, to your advantage. There is an actor called James Bond, a.k.a. 007. He is described as being licensed to kill. This means that in carrying out his official assignment in "Her Majesty's secret service," anybody who becomes a slain victim of the morgue is described as a casualty of war, and James Bond will not be taken before any judge or jury to prove his innocence.

In the same vein as a citizen of the kingdom of God, you have the license to succeed. In the course of carrying out your ambassadorial functions righteously, any obstacle, difficulties, or challenges that you encounter are expected to be victims while you are a victor.

> This people I made especially for myself, a people custom-made to praise me. (Isa. 43:21, MSG)

Heaven has written in you a program that is virus or bugproof. When you run it, the outcome is expected to be righteous success. This is why the Bible says,

> The LORD will defeat your enemies when they attack you. They will attack you from one direction but run away from you in seven directions. (Deut. 28:7, GWT)

The Plan

Since the Holy God is also an excellent God and wants the best for his creation, he had to use the most awesome approach. To realize his plan, he decided to use two of the most powerful offices in the world: kings and priests.

> And hath made us **kings and priests** unto God and his Father; to him be glory and dominion for ever and ever. Amen. (Rev. 1:6, KJV; emphasis added)

While a king's domain and power is mostly terrestrial, the power of a priest is predominantly accessed in the celestial. A king can be likened to the president or prime minister of a nation. A king has the ability to put into effect natural laws, constitutions, or, in some cases, decrees. A priest, on the other hand, has the ability to put into effect spiritual laws and also provide the atmosphere for natural laws to operate.

The king and the priest have their limitations because they are separate entities. Imagine one man effectively holding the same office; such a person can connect and communicate with God (priest), and he can also succeed, promulgate laws and excel on earth (king).

David in the Bible functioned as a king and a priest. Jesus came to perfect the plan, and he excelled as a king and a priest.

In heavenly matters, a priest excels while in earthly matters, a king excels. In some cases, and according to the Bible, you see earthly kings going to priests for assistance or favor (e.g., kings to Elisha). The most appalling situation to God is when a priest vehemently or unashamedly curries the favor of an earthly king for success.

This is somewhat embarrassing to God, and He decided to correct the situation through Jesus Christ by placing the government on his shoulder (king) while the same Jesus also functioned ecclesiastically after the order of Melchizedek (priesthood). The DNA of a king and a priest was in the blood of Jesus.

The Process

In a country like Canada, before you can practice as a medical doctor, nurse, accountant, lawyer, or even drive a car, you must have a license. The license confers on you the ability to practice or "**profess** a good **profess**ion before many witnesses" (1 Tim. 6:12, KJV; emphasis added).

For you to get your driver's license, you would have gone through some training and what is called a road test. This is a practical driving examination to determine your capability to drive a vehicle and your understanding of the various road signs.

When I knew that I was ready to start driving in the province of Ontario, Canada, I requested for an appointment to enable me go through a road test, having passed the written test. The day that I went in for my road test, my examiner sat by my side and told me to drive through a particular route. At a point, we came to a sign that meant, "Do not enter." He did not tell me to take another route but sat still to observe my knowledge of the signs.

I noticed the sign when I approached it and verbally interpreted the sign to him by saying, "Do not enter." He smiled and told me to make a right turn. If I had gone into that road, I am sure that I would have failed the test right there and then. Due to the fact that I passed the test, I was able to get my driver's license.

Do you know that the eyes of the Lord go to and fro to see whose heart is right with him? Concerning a man called David, the Bible says, "the Lord has sought for himself a man after his own heart" (1 Sam. 13:14, NKJV). Every day of our lives, we go through what I will call road tests, and proof that we are ready to get our license is when we do not enter the wide road that leads to destruction but opt for the narrow path. This is when we pass the "road test of life," and the Bible describes this as the following:

> You didn't choose me, but I chose you. I have appointed you to go, to produce fruit that will last, and to ask the Father in my name to give you whatever you ask for. (John 15:16, GWT)

At this time, you receive the License to Succeed because you opted for the way of righteousness. The License to Succeed is available to any man who is ready to make a commitment to the owner of the license. "If any man be in Christ he is a new creature" (2 Cor. 5:17, KJV). This means you have a different genotype and the blood of Jesus is flowing in your veins. The antigens and antibodies in the blood are royalty (kingship) and priesthood.

> But ye are a chosen generation, a royal priesthood, a holy nation, a peculiar people; that ye should shew forth the praises of him who hath called you out of darkness into his marvelous light." (1 Pet. 2:9, KJV)

When the Word of God says you are "a royal priesthood, a holy nation, a peculiar people," it means you can **commune** with heaven, **convey** the communication to the earth, and **conquer** every obstacle.

To be licensed means to be endowed with the right credentials. Anywhere you step into, you have the right credentials to succeed but, above and beyond success, to be significant.

Where confusion becomes the desecrator of some people's license is because they do not know the ETA of their success. The ETA (estimated time of arrival) has already been determined—it is *now*.

God said through the mouth of the prophet Isaiah, "I will do a new thing and NOW it shall spring forth." (Isaiah 43:19) The psalmist said, "NOW is the time to favor Zion, the set time has come." (Psalm 102:13)

Psalm 30:5 says, "Weeping may endure for a night." It is not weeping "will" or "must" endure for a night. It is "may." This definitely means you can determine how long you want to weep (duration). You can put an end to your weeping based on the license that you have.

When Eli, a priest in the Bible, made the prophetic pronouncement concerning Hannah that she will be fruitful by this time next year, she took that word and started chewing on it.

> Your words were found, and I ate them; and Your words were to me a joy and the rejoicing of my heart, for I am called by Your name, O Lord God of hosts. (Jer. 15:16, TAB)

> Your word is very pure (tried and well refined); therefore, Your servant loves it." (Ps. 119:140, TAB)

Utilize the License

No matter the qualifications that you possess, if you do not perform based on what you have, it will just be gathering dust. For a driver who is licensed, despite the fact that he went through the necessary qualification process to get the license in real life, there will still be other cars on the road with different kinds of drivers behind the wheel.

Same thing applies in real life: despite the fact that you are licensed to succeed, situations will still come to check if you have a license, and you will have to tell those situations you do have a license.

> From henceforth let no man trouble me: for I bear in my body the marks of the Lord Jesus. (Gal. 6:17, KJV)

Whatever your challenges are, they do not obfuscate the fact that you are licensed to succeed.

How to Keep Your License

When you look at a licensed driver, the mere fact that he got his license years ago does not confer on him the right to be able to drive forever. There are particular standards that must be kept:

- Maintaining appropriate speed limits
- Checking demerit points
- Ensuring no DUI violations
- Ensuring renewal of license

- Taking emission tests when due
- Others

In the same vein, there are certain things expected of you in the kingdom because your adversary, the devil, is always looking around to see whom he may devour. Though you have victory today does not mean he has left you alone.

> Yesterday's peacock is today's feather duster.

In the lamentations of Jeremiah, he said, "This I recall to my mind, therefore have I hope" (Lam. 3:21, KJV).

You must be able to do a memory recall. Just like computers have random access memory, the below must never be far from your mind whatever the challenges you are facing:

Birth, Not Miscarriage

Birth can be termed as the act or process of bearing or bringing forth offspring or initiating something. It is the physical manifestation of what has been expected but not completely visible. What was visible before birth is the demeanor and physical change of the mother, but nobody could really say to a 100 percent accuracy what the sex, appearance, or status of the offspring would be. A birth puts to rest some of these concerns.

What is noteworthy about birth is that it starts with conception. This involves the union of a male and female. While the expectant mother goes about sometimes through a measure of discomfort, at the same time, there is an inner glow—an inner glow, because she will be a conduit for the commencement of another life. The experience of women differs while pregnant, but the expectations of most are the same.

> And Sarah declared, "God has brought me laughter. All who hear about this will laugh with me." (Gen. 21:6, NLT)

While the woman is pregnant, she may have visited prenatal clinics, and while the doctor may have mentioned a probable time of delivery, it is still a probable date, it is not certain. You can liken the life of a Christian to the process of birth—being born again. Almost all living beings are trying to

The License

birth one thing or the other, but what most do not know is when, which is a function of time.

A whole lot of believers are apprehensive as to when they will see the birth or the physical manifestation of the promises of God in their life. A critical point of note is that everything in life is a process.

For the physical birth of a baby or offspring, there is union (male and female), pregnancy, confirmation, symptoms (sickness, discomfort), progression, preparation, birth, and then celebration. The same thing applies to anything of note you will ever achieve in life. You may conceive it, but it has to be properly incubated so that it will not be premature or a stillbirth. When we become apprehensive about any situation, we begin to ask many questions, even questioning the giver of the promise. Those who are able to quickly put to rest any lingering doubt are those who readily affirm who they are in Jesus.

When you completely surrender to Him, He will do more than any parent for you. God is able to redeem you from shame and, in exchange, give you a part of his glory.

> But God will redeem my life from the grave; he will surely take me to himself. (Ps. 49:15, NIV)

In the goodness and infinite mercy of God, He saved you from destruction. When you were dead in your sins, He redeemed you. To redeem means to recover ownership. This implies you were formerly owned by the devil through the avenue of sin, and a recovery had to be done. This recovery took a huge process. If you own something, before you bought that thing, it must have some worth, and it must be relatively precious when it was bought.

When you were in the camp of the devil, you were precious to the kingdom of darkness to help in furthering the work of darkness and derailing those who are in the light. Do you know what? Some really succeeded in getting recruits into the enemy's camp and making a shipwreck of the faith of some who were believers in Christ.

At a point in time, you were mired in the clay of destruction and defeat. Despite all those things you were doing then, one thing you did not know was that Satan, who was then your master, had been defeated because Jesus Christ pronounced that he saw Satan falling down as lightning from the sky.

You were also, in effect, defeated by reason of association with the devil and all his practices.

You were actually losing while you erroneously believed that you were winning. You saw yourselves as a success. As many as are in the devil's camp have been programmed for destruction, the only thing that has been keeping them going is that God, in His mercy, has not allowed them to press the destruct button yet.

The good thing is that some opted, by the grace of God, for the button of life at the time it had been appointed because a decision was made when it pleased the Most High God to buy them back.

> But when it pleased God, who separated me from my mother's womb and called me through His grace. (Gal. 1:15, NKJV)

To buy back implied a higher price had to be paid by the one doing the buyback. The price was the blood of Jesus.

> For you know that God paid a ransom to save you from the empty life you inherited from your ancestors. And the ransom he paid was not mere gold or silver. It was the precious blood of Christ, the sinless, spotless Lamb of God. (1 Pet. 1:18–19, NLT)

It took Jesus laying down His life and shedding his blood, because the life of the flesh is in the blood. Let me expand more on the concept of buyback. In the days of slavery, when a master buys a slave, he brands the slave. In some cases, a sort of mark was placed on the body of the slave to make sure they only eat when he wanted them to eat. A hole was made in the upper and lower lip, and a padlock was used to seal their mouths.

When you were bought back, all these marks were eliminated, and a new mark was placed upon you that identifies whom you belong to.

> But the firm foundation of (laid by) God stands, sure and unshaken, bearing this seal (inscription): The Lord knows those who are His, and, Let everyone who names [himself by] the name of the Lord give up all iniquity and stand aloof from it. (2 Tim. 2:19, TAB)

This new mark not only announces to whom you belong but also wards off enemies from attacking you.

> From henceforth let no man trouble me: for I bear in my body the marks of the Lord Jesus. (Gal. 6:17, KJV)

Jesus did not only redeem or buy you back, but he also rescued you from defeat. In a competition where medals—gold, silver, and bronze—are given, the persons who are first, second, and third get the aforementioned medals respectively. There are some key things: the other participants do not get any medal, and they do not mount the podium. The ones who won stand on the higher podium.

The above example is in a competition that involves more than two. In the competition between the kingdom of darkness and light, the winner takes it all. The good thing is that Jesus had already taken it all, hallelujah! After he was crucified on the cross and put in the tomb, he went to hades, sheol, and took the keys of death and hell from the devil. He also freed all the patriarchs who had been held in captivity. This is why the Word of God can say, "Death, where is your sting, and, grave, where is your victory?" Jesus Christ redeemed you into the winning camp and rescued you from defeat. You have been raised to sit in heavenly places with Christ Jesus far above principalities and powers.

A whole lot of people have cried and cried, attributing their situation to the fact that they did not surrender their life to Jesus on time. An apostle also had this same problem, because there was a time he was recounting his life to the people of Corinth, and he said, "And last of all He appeared to me also, as to one prematurely and born dead [no better than an unperfected fetus among living men]" (1 Cor. 15:8, TAB).

When he had the chance to truly re-examine his life, he changed his confession:

> But when He, Who had chosen and set me apart [even] before I was born and had called me by His grace (His undeserved favor and blessing), saw fit and was pleased to reveal (unveil, disclose) His Son within me so that I might proclaim Him among the Gentiles (the non-Jewish world) as the glad tidings (Gospel), immediately I did not confer with flesh and blood [did not consult or counsel with any

frail human being or communicate with anyone]. (Gal. 1:15–16, TAB)

You should not be crying about when you gave your life to Christ or became born again (i.e., received the license to succeed as if you were born out of time). It was when it pleased the Lord that He separated you unto himself. If you take time to carefully study the Word of God, you would see an insight being given:

> You didn't choose me, remember; I chose you, and put you in the world to bear fruit, fruit that won't spoil. As fruit bearers, whatever you ask the Father in relation to me, he gives you. (John 15:16, MSG)

In reality, maybe you hearkened to an altar call, or you somehow surrendered to receive the life that only Jesus Christ gives, but it was God who made it happen at the time designated. He was the one who decided you need the license to succeed.

The reason for the choice is also mentioned—to bear fruit. The psalmist said, "Why art thou cast down O my soul, put your hope in the Lord."

It is about putting your hope not in the shame of the past but in the glory of the future.

> I knew you before I formed you in your mother's womb. Before you were born I set you apart and appointed you as my prophet to the nations. (Jer. 1:5, NLT)

If God knew you before you were formed in your mother's womb, it means He had also designated a time for you to be born. How can you then be a miscarriage? No matter the pain associated with your birth, that is how He wanted it to happen. You are birthed into the way of righteousness for the license to succeed not miscarried for misfortune. You have to continually say this phrase to yourself no matter the odds of life that is stacked against you—I am birthed not miscarried. It is also extremely important that you do not just verbalize it but believe it and behave it. This must show in your actions. Hannah believed the words of prophet Eli regarding having a baby and her countenance was no longer sad. She even went to eat.

The License

> Jabez was a better man than his brothers, a man of honor. His mother had named him Jabez (Oh, the pain!), saying, "A painful birth! I bore him in great pain!" (1 Chron. 4:9, MSG)

Forget the travail, shame, etc., associated with your birth, and focus on what God is doing. You cannot keep on regretting your past without regressing your future. You were birthed, not miscarried.

What if you made a mistake after giving your life to Christ (i.e., after you received the license to succeed) then go back to him and totally confess your sins and shun them? Make sure you do not go back to them. Do you know there is recognition that you can make mistakes? But you should not be living a life of mistakes.

This statement is not an authorization for you to do whatever you like and then attribute it to mistakes:

> My little children, for whom I am again suffering birth pangs until Christ is completely and permanently formed (molded) within you. (Gal. 4:19, NKJV)

If you have genuinely repented of any past sin, God is able to graft you in again.

> And don't get to feeling superior to those pruned branches down on the ground. If they don't persist in remaining deadwood, they could very well get grafted back in. God can do that. He can perform miracle grafts. (Rom. 11:23, MSG)

Let us use the illustration of a driver who contravened the traffic laws or was involved in an accident. Depending on the traffic code violated or the number of kilometers he was over the speed limit, he could have demerit points or his license suspended. This will lead to paying a higher insurance premium.

Though there is a consequence for traffic-code violation, it does not outrightly lead to a withdrawal of your driving privileges. But know this carefully. You cannot continue to violate traffic code and not expect to subsequently have your driving license withdrawn. Neither can you continue to bash your car after repeated visits to the mechanic or body shop and not have the car grounded or operating in a deformed state.

So it is with you. You cannot continue in sin and expect grace to abound. You need to ensure you desist from sin.

2

Your DNA

An unmistakable attribute that exists between you and your senior brother and saviour, Jesus, is the light.

> Once more Jesus addressed the crowd. He said, I am the Light of the world. He who follows Me will not be walking in the dark, but will have the Light which is Life. (John 8:12, TAB)

Jesus was and is still described as the Light of the world, and you are also described as the light of the world.

> You are the light of the world—like a city on a hilltop that cannot be hidden. No one lights a lamp and then puts it under a basket. Instead, a lamp is placed on a stand, where it gives light to everyone in the house. In the same way, let your good deeds shine out for all to see, so that everyone will praise your heavenly Father. (Matt. 5:14–16, NLT)

This definitely means that when you become a kingdom citizen, His "will or inheritance" left for you says you become light. I used to think that as an ambassador of Jesus Christ, a kingdom citizen and an inheritor of His glorious will, that I am a light carrier, but he did not say that. He said, "I am the light of the world." This is mind-blowing.

What is seen in the physical is not what all the spiritual forces, both negative and positive, see.

This means as a carrier of the kingdom passport with the license to succeed—a new name that not only identifies me on my passport but also announces me is light. While there is no controversy about Jesus describing himself as the light but concerning you, the inheritors of his will, you have been advised in his will to let your light shine. It is only when you present yourself as light that you can continue to shine.

The light that you emit causes others to come and take refuge under the umbrella of your glow or radiation, and the one who has made it possible for you to be approved as a kingdom citizen despite the darkness that you used to embody is then recognized and praised.

This definitely means that what will certify that you receive the benefits as contained in his will is letting your light to shine, not hiding it. As Jesus Christ functioned appropriately as the Light of the world, so also must you.

You have something very important that Jesus has in his DNA: light. Your DNA is light. If you are able to operate according to your constitution without deviation, then all those around you will definitely see your light and give glory to the Almighty Father.

Arise [from the depression and prostration in which circumstances have kept you—rise to a new life]! Shine (be radiant with the glory of the Lord), for your light has come, and the glory of the Lord has risen upon you! (Isaiah 60:1, TAB; Classic)

What Is DNA?

Deoxyribonucleic acid (DNA) is a nucleic acid that contains the genetic instructions used in the development and functioning of living organisms. The main role of DNA molecules is the long-term storage of information. DNA is often compared to a set of blueprints, like a recipe or a code, since it contains the instructions needed to construct other components of cells. Other DNA sequences have structural purposes or are involved in regulating the use of this genetic information.

There are various keywords in the definition of DNA: instructions, development, functioning, long-term storage of information, set of blueprints, structural purposes, and regulation. In any first world, developing, or lawful society, these keywords are not only present but also part of the fabric of the society. You will see structure, regulation, instruction, development, functioning, blueprints (how-to), and long-term storage of information.

You must also have these keywords as functional attributes for a successful life despite the fact that you possess the license to succeed.

Instruction (what to do): Jesus, while teaching the crowd in Jerusalem, said,

> I have never spoken on My own authority or of My own accord or as self-appointed, but the Father Who sent Me has Himself given Me orders [concerning] what to say and what to tell. And I know that His commandment is (means) eternal life. So whatever I speak, I am saying [exactly] what My Father has told Me to say and in accordance with His instructions. (John 12:49–50, TAB)

Despite what can be acclaimed as the power or authority of Jesus, he said, "I follow instructions." This definitely demonstrates the importance of the ability to comply with laid-down instructions for a life of enduring success.

Here are guidelines for those with the license to succeed:

- No one with the license to succeed is ever self-appointed (you have not chosen me, but I have chosen you—John 15:16).
- If the one whom you want to inherit from says he follows instruction, then for you to be a partaker of the divine inheritance, you also need to follow instruction.
- It is the authority of the one whom you obey that confers authority on you and makes every other thing to also obey you.
- It is not only about carrying out the instruction but also how you carry out the instruction.
- You do not add nor subtract from his instructions.

Jesus Christ followed not only verbal but also pictorial and appropriate behavioral instructions.

> So Jesus explained himself at length. "I'm telling you this straight. The Son can't independently do a thing, only what he sees the Father doing. What the Father does, the Son does." (John 5:19, MSG)

As you possess the license to succeed, you should never forget that you are a kingdom ambassador. No kingdom ambassador is independent of the kingdom. Every kingdom ambassador is an appendage of the King.

Appendage, when looked at in the extreme, can be subjective, but in the as-is interpretation, it simply means somebody or something that is dependent on another.

In botany, it is defined as any subsidiary part of a plant, such as a branch or leaf.

In anatomy, it is a part or organ attached to a main structure and subordinate in function or size.

Every kingdom ambassador is expected to just carry out the instruction of the King, not look for ways to circumvent the instructions.

> Do not think that I have come to do away with or undo the Law or the Prophets; I have come not to do away with or undo but to complete and fulfill them. (Matt. 5:17, TAB)

Granted, you have been given the capacity to think (because it takes you to the realm of possibilities so as to nullify every impossibility if the right kingdom secrets are applied), but when it comes to kingdom instructions as contained in the will of your senior brother and saviour—Jesus, you just obey them.

The obedience of the instructions sets aside the law of sin and death and causes the law of the spirit of life in Christ Jesus to begin to operate on your behalf.

Due to the fact that your senior brother was carrying out the instructions (verbal and behavioral) of His Father, He started looking like Him. They became one.

> You've been with me all this time, Philip, and you still don't understand? *To see me is to see the Father.* So how can you ask, "Where is the Father?" Don't you believe that I am in the Father and the Father is in me? The words that I speak

> to you aren't mere words. I don't just make them up on my own. The Father who resides in me crafts each word into a divine act. (John 14:9–10, MSG)

If you also completely adhere to His instructions, you will begin to look like Him, and He will begin to craft every one of your words into divine act.

> I assure you, most solemnly I tell you, if anyone steadfastly believes in Me, he will himself be able to do the things that I do; and he will do even greater things than these, because I go to the Father. (John 14:12, TAB)

Instruction is the impartation of knowledge. This can be achieved through training, lessons, or reorientation. An instruction is a detailed direction on procedure. It describes how something can be done or the means through which an objective can be attained.

Instruction can come in the form of a statement, an advice, or a command. King Solomon laid emphasis on instruction:

> Listen, my child, to what your father teaches you. Don't neglect your mother's teaching. What you learn from them will crown you with grace and clothe you with honor. (Prov. 1:8–9, NLT)

When you put into practice what you have been taught, you are crowned with favor and clothed with honor. Since instruction when imbibed leads to understanding, it in effect means that, an understanding of what you have to do will make you outstanding—an understanding of the fact that the life cycle of an annual plant differs from a perennial plant and the worth of a cash crop differs from a food crop turns you to a success.

Henri Frederic Amiel said, "What is an intelligent man? A man who enters with ease and completeness into the spirit of things and the intention of persons, and who arrives at an end by the shortest route."

When you are instructed on a matter, situation, or circumstance, you are being thoroughly equipped to know what to do before, during, and after you face the situation. You thereby enter with ease and completeness into the spirit of the situation.

A wonderful analogy is what a good coach goes through in preparing his wards for a match. The coach would study the opposing team, collect data, and study their reaction to different situations. An in-depth study of the individuals in the team will also be done. This information will now be passed to his team in the form of instruction, training, or coaching.

I once read about how a boxing coach told his ward (Helen the Kitten) that all you have to do is make sure you jab the face of the opponent (Kathy the Cat) because she swells easily. The lady followed the instruction, and she won.

When you follow divine instruction, you become a divine champion, and you reap divine harvest.

> And Elisha said, "Borrow as many empty jars as you can from your friends and neighbors. Then go into your house with your sons and shut the door behind you. Pour olive oil from your flask into the jars, setting the jars aside as they are filled." When she told the man of God what had happened, he said to her, "Now sell the olive oil and pay your debts, and there will be enough money left over to support you and your sons." (2 Kings 4:3–7, NLT)

The woman in the above story came to meet Elijah with a problem: debt. The solution proffered by the man of God involved borrowing, but the woman did not complain. She complied with all the instructions given. She was told to borrow from friends and neighbors. Despite her poverty, she had friends. If she had no friends, there will be fewer people to borrow from.

The next instruction was that she should shut the door with her sons. When she did all these tasks, she still went to the man of God to know what to do with the harvest. She moved from a borrower to a seller. She ultimately became a treasurer for God, a good custodian of the harvest all because of instruction. Never run away from good and wholesome instructions.

> A wise man will hear and will increase learning; and a man of understanding shall attain unto wise counsels. (Prov. 1:5, KJV)

One thing that is not in doubt is divine enablement to carry out instructions. This year, heaven will help you in Jesus's name, amen.

> Then the LORD said to Elijah, "Go and live in the village of Zarephath, near the city of Sidon. There is a widow there who will feed you. I have given her my instructions." (1 Kings 17:8-9, NLT)

Consider first the dilemma of Elijah based on the instruction given to him—go and stay with a widow. A lady without a husband? God, are you sure? What will people say? Elijah could conclude that this is Satan at work—an instruction like this can never be from God but he complied.

The next hurdle that Elijah had to cross was arriving at the widow's house and the widow really had nothing to offer. This widow had a little just enough for her and her son, but God said I have given an instruction for the widow to feed you. Elijah could be contemplating the following in his mind—God, you must have sent me to the wrong widow especially when the widow even verbalized that she had nothing.

You must never forget in life that the ways of God are a mystery. I must also warn that this does not mean that you should not be guided in your dealings with others. Maybe you are a counsellor, ensure that all measures are in place to prevent your fall into temptation. Do not say Elijah did it and you go and start living with a widow.

We must also not forget the actions of the widow. The widow was able to obey the divine instruction because of the assistance of heaven. She sacrificially gave her last meal for abundant life. When the instruction seems difficult, Jehovah El Shaddai will sustain you.

Instructions and How to Handle Them

We can say that the Bible or the will of the King or the kingdom laws are filled with instructions that can be sometimes challenging to fulfill, but when you take time to reflect on those instructions, you will find out that submitting to them will guarantee success, and also prolong your length of days on this earth.

Let us review some instructions:

Do Not Worry (Insults and Troubles Are Raw Materials)

As kingdom citizens and members of the commonwealth of Israel, there are certain things or expectations from you to not only keep your citizenship but also enjoy the benefits. As a Canadian citizen, the benefit that you enjoy is different from that of a landed immigrant, refugee claimant, or illegal immigrant. For example, a Canadian citizen can go to many nations of the world without a visa, a landed immigrant can only go to most nations with a visa, and a refugee claimant or applicant has limited access to benefits of the nation and is not expected to even leave the country while an illegal immigrant lives in fear of deportation.

As heirs of the Father and joint heirs of the Son, we sometimes behave not as citizens of the kingdom but, in the worst scenario, an illegal immigrant. Consider the situation illustrated in the book of Nehemiah:

> They told me, "Those who survived captivity are in the province. *They are enduring serious troubles and being insulted.* The wall of Jerusalem has broken down, and its gates have been destroyed by fire." (Neh. 1:3, GWT)

It is important that you know that the one who heard the news is called Nehemiah, an exile. Even in exile, he had a position or an office that could be deemed as dangerous, but he eventually became distinct by his attitude.

I was a cupbearer to the king at this time. (Neh. 1:11, GWT)

It is interesting to note that the Bible did not say, "He was a cupbearer to the king." A phrase "at this time" became the trailer. He knew his present state would not be his future or forever state. I want to prophesy into your destiny that your present state, with all its challenges, will not be your descriptor forever. The tide will turn for you positively in Jesus's name.

In the olden days, when you are a cupbearer, you are not only expected to bring the choice drinks for the king but also to do it with a cheerful face and ensure the drinks are free from impurities (e.g., poison). His position could elicit reprimand or instant death, depending on the whim of the king.

The news that this "cupbearer at this time" called Nehemiah heard was a progression from commendable to depressing:

- It started with, "Those who survived the captivity are in the province." When the nation of Israel was attacked by the Medes and Persians, some were killed, some were maimed and eventually died, while others who were seen as viable (intellectually, economically, and socially) were taken to Susa (presently in modern-day Iran). In this context, to survive wasn't too bad a thing because, "[There is no exemption] but he who is joined to all the living has hope—for a living dog is better than a dead lion" (Eccles. 9:4, TAB).
- The second part of the above statement says, "Are in the province." Though they were survivors, there are still certain laws that guide their residency in that province. As a resident of the province of Ontario, there are dos and don'ts. I am expected to be law-abiding, to pay taxes. If I have a house during the winter, I am expected to plough my driveway. When I get to the red light, even if there are no police cruisers or cameras, I am expected to stop. I should observe the speed limit. Failure to adhere to these laws has serious consequences once I decide I want to live in Canada and stay in the province. No matter where you have found yourself, there are certain laws—both physical and spiritual—that govern "your province." Take time to discover the laws.
- They are enduring serious troubles and being insulted. This statement in itself is not that bad, but it exemplifies the lifestyle of people with average or below-average mentality. Though they are enduring, the expectation is for them to live above the troubles and insults. You have the power to stop enduring and to start excelling. A typical example is the mentality that has ruined many marriages. Marriages were designed by God to be enjoyed not endured.
- "The wall of Jerusalem has broken down and its gates have been destroyed by fire." They allowed their protection, defense, and the control of egress and exit to be taken away from them. They allowed their challenges to overwhelm and suppress them. When you stay too long in the toilet of affliction, different pernicious vermin will eventually crawl out of the woodwork and attack you.

Every promise of God has as its hypostasis his principles (i.e., promises follows or stands on principles).

When Nehemiah got the disturbing news, he did not allow it to derail him. He allowed his light to shine. He did something in spite of his state:

> Lord please pay attention to my prayer and to the prayers of all your other servants who want to worship your name. Please give me success today and make this man, King Artaxerxes, show me compassion. I was cupbearer to the king at this time. (Neh. 1:11, GWT)

When you keep on giving excuses to subvert or escape the instructions of God, you will eventually excuse away your glorious future.

As a member of a functioning province, you cannot tell a police officer that the reason why you ran the red light is because you just had a disagreement with your husband, wife, or business partner and your mind was not on what you were doing (simply having challenges). I am sure the police officer could empathize with you but he will also let you know, based on your reason (s), that you are not supposed to be driving because you are a danger to the society.

Due to certain things that you are holding on to in real life, as kingdom citizens and members of the commonwealth of Israel, you become a danger not only to yourself but also to other citizens.

There are certain expectations in the testament of the kingdom that governs worries and concerns. If you do not follow the instruction for handling worries, you become a danger to yourself, destiny, family, business, community, the church of God, and other kingdom citizens. When you are able to understand that your wealthy (in all its ramifications) brother died and he left a will for you (the Bible), and that this will covers every solution to every situation you are facing or will encounter, you become better.

In His will or inheritance, He said,

> Casting the whole of your care [all your anxieties, all your worries, all your concerns, once and for all] on Him, for He cares for you affectionately and cares about you watchfully. (1 Pet. 5:7, TAB)

Jesus advised his disciples (such advice is still relevant in your situation today) to stop worrying about the necessities of life. He went on to say that life is more than those things. Some people have so much worried about their business, children, food, etc., that they have invited deadly and destiny-destroying ailments into their lives.

I once had a discussion with someone, and she said, "I do not know what has become of me." The reality is that, this individual allowed worries and the fear of tomorrow to take a stranglehold upon her. Fear torments.

> Don't be afraid little flock. Your father is pleased to give you the kingdom. (Luke 12:32, GWT)

What He is pleased to give you is righteousness (right standing with him), peace (wholeness, nothing missing or broken), and joy in the Holy Ghost (joy of the Lord that strengthens to hear the inaudible, see the invisible, and do the impossible).

If you run afoul of the instruction of how to handle your worries as laid down in the will of your Saviour—Jesus, you do not get anything from his inheritance. What you eventually get are ulcers, depression, etc., which are not from him.

Also, when you are supposed to yearly renew the sticker on your car and pay your insurance, you cannot tell the judge the reason why you are unable to pay is because your expenses have gone up. I am sure the judge will tell you that if you want to continue to drive your car, you need to reduce your expenses, else you will lose the privilege of driving. In the province of Ontario, the penalty for driving without insurance is $5,000. This tells me that when you run afoul of earthly law in a lawful society, there are penalties.

In the kingdom of God, as also laid down in the will of our Saviour—Jesus, there are penalties for disobeying the rule that governs the different situations that we face. When we refuse to pay kingdom insurance (tithes) due to one excuse or the other, we open ourselves to devourers, and we also lose some of our privileges as citizens and ambassadors of the commonwealth of Israel.

When you follow His instructions, principles, and precepts as laid down in his will of how to face any situation that you encounter, you compel the hand of God to move on your behalf. It was because David diligently took care of the sheep that God sought him out in the wilderness. Esther was able to not only submit but also follow simple instruction: "Do not disclose who you are." Noah was living right before God, and he became a candidate for favor.

In any situation you find yourself, it is extremely important to note that God is there:

> The Lord was with Joseph, so he became a successful man. He worked in the house of his Egyptian master. (Gen. 39:2, GWT)

> While Joseph was in prison, the Lord was with him. The Lord reached out to him with his unchanging love and gave him protection. The Lord also put Joseph on good terms with the warden. (Gen. 39:21–22, GWT)

The troubles and insults from his brothers and Potiphar's wife were all turned into raw materials. Not once did the Bible say that he was worried. In the house of his Egyptian master, he was serving faithfully. In the prison, he was helping others. Even after interpreting the dream for the butler and the butler forgot all about him, Joseph knew there was an appointed time and an acceptable year.

When the acceptable time, lines up with the acceptable year in the life of an accepted man (with the license for success), there will be accelerated achievement.

It is important that you observe the laid-down instructions of the kingdom in the time of difficulties. The content of the will says,

> I have told you these things, so that in Me you may have [perfect] peace and confidence. In the world you have tribulation and trials and distress and frustration; but be of good cheer [take courage; be confident, certain, undaunted]! For I have overcome the world. [I have deprived it of power to harm you and have conquered it for you.] (John 16:33, TAB)

If He has told you these things, it behooves you to adhere because faith comes by hearing, and "He that has an ear, let him hear." You have the choice to obey the letters of the inheritance if you want to benefit from it. If you adhere, there will be perfect peace and confidence, but failure to do so results in tribulations and trials.

This is telling you that, if you think you have troubles, you have not seen anything yet if you do not approach it appropriately, because trouble is a family. In the family of troubles, you have frustration, depression, division, tribulation, trials, distress, etc.

If your pain is economic (i.e., cash flow), if you do not follow the letters of the will to handle the situation—"Thou will keep him in perfect peace whose mind is stayed on thee because he trusts in thee" (Isa. 26:3, KJV) and "My God shall supply all my needs according to His riches in glory" (Phil. 4:19, KJV)—you may eventually develop health problems.

In whatever represents economic or financial problems, the guidance of God through applying the correct and ethical business principles can get you out of the problem. The solution that you did not see before can be revealed for you to get out of the mess. God opened the eyes of Hagar to see a well even in her sorrow (Genesis 21:19).

The woman with the issue of blood went to several physicians, but she did not get better until she went to the physician of physicians.

> Consider it a sheer gift, friends, when tests and challenges come at you from all sides. You know that under pressure, your faith-life is forced into the open and shows its true colors. (James 1:2, MSG)

If you are able to understand that your challenges are gifts, then you know how to process those challenges to work for you.

> A man's gift makes room for him and brings him before great men. (Prov. 18:16, TAB)

You need to realize that examination is not a problem. Any student that treats examination as a problem will never be promoted. Examinations always require a period of preparation for there to be promotion. Therefore, the challenges that you are facing are examinations and if you pass, you will be promoted.

Second instruction to look at is **Anger.** Consider how the manual for excellent living instructs you to handle anger:

> Do not be quick in spirit to be angry or vexed, for anger and vexation lodge in the bosom of fools. (Eccles. 7:9, TAB)

Everyone, to a certain extent, struggles with anger. While some people accept and take responsibility for their anger to contain and creatively channel it into a positive energy, others sadly justify their anger, and even shift or spread the blame for their action on some others. They say, "It is because he did something to me that I responded in such a way."

This next statement I am about to make may sound controversial, but a major reason why you get angry is because the instruction for creating the act called anger is present in your DNA. Do you know that God the Almighty, the Jehovah Elohim (Your Creator) gets angry? Here are some verses in the Bible that show just that:

> The Lord was so angry with Aaron that he wanted to destroy him, too. But I prayed for Aaron, and the Lord spared him. (Deut. 9:20, NLT)

> The Lord was very angry with Solomon, for his heart had turned away from the Lord, the God of Israel, who had appeared to him twice. (1 Kings 11:9, NLT)

> God is an honest judge. He is angry with the wicked every day. (Ps. 7:11, NLT)

The Hebrew word for anger is *kuf-ayin-samech*, or *ka'as* for short. This could either mean anger or sorrow, and this word is used interchangeably. In many parts of the Bible where you see God's anger, it could actually mean sorrow.

Contrast the two translations below:

> He looked them in the eye, one after another, angry now, furious at their hard-nosed religion. He said to the man, "Hold out your hand." He held it out—it was as good as new! (Mark 3:5, MSG)

> He looked around at them angrily and was deeply saddened by their hard hearts. Then he said to the man, "Hold out

your hand." So the man held out his hand, and it was restored! (Mark 3:5, NLT)

Two Greek words are used in the New Testament for *anger*. One means "passion, energy" and the other means "agitated, boiling."

According to kingdom constitution, anger is God-given energy intended to help you solve problems. Since you are created in His image, He knows you will be angry, but He now instructed in His will or kingdom constitution *how* to be angry:

> And don't sin by letting anger control you. Don't let the sun go down while you are still angry, for anger gives a foothold to the devil. (Eph. 4:26–27, NLT)

He knows the energy from anger could either be positively or negatively channeled. When negatively channeled, it could be destructive, but if positively channeled, it could be creative. Whether positive or negative, anger can alter a man's destiny.

Anger can shatter communication and tear apart relationships, and it ruins both the joy and health of many.

The contrasting outcome of anger:

	Negative outcome of anger	Positive outcome of anger
1.	Self-defense	Principle defense
2.	Selfishness	Selflessness
3.	Personality attack	Problem attack
4.	Multiplies hurt	Multiplies love
5.	Uncontrolled and rude emotion	Controlled and respectful utterance
6.	Lingers to malice and depression	Process to improve and excel
7.	Unrelated outbursts	Unified outcome
8.	Return evil with abundant evil	Return evil with abundant good

When you exhibit anger negatively,

You make yourself equal to God (Isa. 30:27, 30), negating the instructions in His will that says, "Vengeance is mine, I will repay says the Lord."

Other reasons why you cannot get angry the way God gets angry despite the fact you have been created in His image are:

- He is Omnipotent (He is all-powerful), Omniscient (He is all-knowing), and Omnipresent (He is everywhere).
- He is the same yesterday, today, and forever—He does not change.
- No matter how good you are, you are still a mere mortal.
- He is the only one that can kill and make alive.
- If He gets angry and destroys, just by one word, He can recreate.
- He can be angry with a man or a nation and at the same time be blessing another man or nation.
- You portray that you do not believe God or His will for your life. (Heb. 4:2)
- You demonstrate that you know more than him (Isaiah 45:9)

The next instruction that needs careful consideration is **Forgiveness:**

> And forgive us our debts, as we also have forgiven (left, remitted, and let go of the debts, and have given up resentment against) our debtors. For if you forgive people their trespasses [their reckless and willful sins, leaving them, letting them go, and giving up resentment], your heavenly Father will also forgive you. (Matt. 6:12, 14, TAB)

Forgiveness is therapeutic because it brings healing and refreshment.

> And behold, they brought to Him a man paralyzed and prostrated by illness, lying on a sleeping pad; and when Jesus saw their faith, He said to the paralyzed man, "Take courage, son; your sins are forgiven, and the penalty remitted." (Matt. 9:2, TAB)

When you forgive the wrong of others, you actually free yourself from carrying an undeserved burden. The heaviness of the spirit is lightened.

Lack of forgiveness can kill not only physically but also spiritually.

> So [instead of further rebuke, now] you should rather turn and [graciously] forgive and comfort and encourage [him],

> to keep him from being overwhelmed by excessive sorrow
> and despair. (2 Cor. 2:7, TAB)

As kingdom citizens with the license to succeed, you have as part of your DNA the instruction for forgiveness because the one who created you has forgiveness as one of his attributes.

> To the Lord our God belong mercy and loving-kindness
> and forgiveness. (Dan. 9:9a, TAB)

The "letters of the will" left for you in the Bible says you should even forgive in impossible situations.

> And Jesus prayed, Father, forgive them, for they know not
> what they do. And they divided His garments and distributed
> them by casting lots for them. (Luke 23:34, TAB)

To get anything from His inheritance, He advised that forgiveness should be continuous.

> Then Peter came up to Him and said, Lord, how many
> times may my brother sin against me and I forgive him and
> let it go? [As many as] up to seven times? Jesus answered
> him, I tell you, not up to seven times, but seventy times
> seven! (Matt. 18:21–22, TAB)

Forgiveness will lead to another instruction, which implies you are offering something—**Giving.** When you forgive somebody a wrongdoing, you are actually giving or offering an avenue for healing or a renewal of relationship.

This is an instruction that a lot of kingdom citizens know but refuse to obey. This is because they believe that whatever they have most—especially their money—is by their power, but the kingdom handbook says,

> If you start thinking to yourselves, "I did all this; And
> all by myself; I'm rich; It's all mine!"—well, think again.
> Remember that GOD, your God, gave you the strength
> to produce all this wealth so as to confirm the covenant
> that he promised to your ancestors—as it is today. (Deut.
> 8:17–18, MSG)

The ability to go to work whether you are an employer or employee is by the strength of God. What happens if you cannot go to that job again? For a lot of people, the source of income will definitely dry up. It is important you honor the one who gives you the ability to produce the wealth.

> John answered, "A man can receive nothing [he can claim nothing, he can take unto himself nothing] except as it has been granted to him from heaven. [A man must be content to receive the gift which is given him from heaven; there is no other source.]" (John 3:27, TAB)

Giving is not about convenience. This will be a tough one to handle for some. Once again, giving is not according to convenience or when you think you have the ability or wherewithal. You have been instructed to give. I want you to know I am not trying to hoodwink you or wind you up, but I have come to understand this principle of kingdom return on investment because it is a spiritual transaction.

> Then Isaac sowed seed in that land and received in the same year a hundred times as much as he had planted, and the Lord favored him with blessings. And the man became great and gained more and more until he became very wealthy and distinguished. (Gen. 26:12–13, TAB)

Some of the considerations about the above passage have always been, "Where did Isaac get the seed to sow, considering the fact there was dearth? Why did he not turn his seed to bread?" (This is a ready alternative to a lot of kingdom citizens: when "they believe" that they do not have enough, they turn their seed to bread.)

Such an action readily contravenes kingdom laws and its code of conduct because there is a difference between seed and bread.

> For as the rain and snow come down from the heavens, and return not there again, but water the earth and make it bring forth and sprout, that it may give seed to the sower and bread to the eater. (Isa. 55:10, TAB)

As seed is always available, so is bread. You, therefore, need to make a choice whether you want your seed to produce bread so you can eat and also be a supplier, or you want to eat your seed as bread. If you decide to eat your seed as bread, it simply means that very soon there might not be bread for you to eat. You would have devoured the avenue or the process of providing more bread.

While seed multiplies, bread diminishes. It is only a seed that can reproduce, but bread cannot because it is seedless. While a seed can produce bread, bread cannot produce seed.

> <u>This most generous God who gives seed to the farmer that becomes bread for your meals</u> is more than extravagant with you. He gives you something you can then give away, which grows into full-formed lives, robust in God, wealthy in every way, so that you can be generous in every way, producing with us great praise to God. (2 Cor. 9:10–11, MSG; emphasis added)

It is fitting to refer to God as the "only wise God." The King of the kingdom already tried this principle when He "gave His only begotten Son." This is an example of generous and sacrificial giving.

> They who sow in tears shall reap in joy and singing. (Ps. 126:5, TAB)

Though tithing is part of giving and the kingdom instruction commands us to do that, we are also told the following:

> "Bring all the tithes into the storehouse so there will be enough food in my Temple. If you do," says the Lord of Heaven's Armies. "I will open the windows of heaven for you. I will pour out a blessing so great you won't have enough room to take it in! Try it! Put me to the test!" (Mal. 3:10, TAB)

But tithing is actually the beginning of giving. If you are tithing, may the Lord cause His promises to come true for you as you obey His instructions, but note that as much as you have the ability, you should do more so that you can get to the realm of giving.

> He who observes the wind [and waits for all conditions to be favorable] will not sow, and he who regards the clouds will not reap. (Eccles. 11:4, TAB)

Many struggle with tithing but in many verses in the book of Hebrews, you will see Jesus Christ being referred to as a priest after the order of Melchizedek.

As an example, "For those who formerly became priests received their office without its being confirmed by the taking of an oath by God, but this One was designated and addressed and saluted with an oath, The Lord has sworn and will not regret it *or* change His mind, You are a Priest forever *according to the order of Melchizedek.*" (Hebrews 7:21, TAB; Classic)

If Jesus Christ is made a priest forever after the order of Melchizedek, you then find out who was Melchizedek in the Bible. Let us go to the book of Genesis to discover that.

Melchizedek king of Salem [later called Jerusalem] brought out bread and wine [for their nourishment]; he was the priest of God Most High, **19** And he blessed him and said, Blessed (favored with blessings, made blissful, joyful) be Abram by God Most High, Possessor *and* Maker of heaven and earth, **20** And blessed, praised, *and* glorified be God Most High, Who has given your foes into your hand! And [Abram] gave him a tenth of all [he had taken]. (Genesis 14:18-20, TAB; Classic)

From the above you then know a couple of things about Melchizedek:

- He brought out bread and wine
- He blessed Abraham
- Abraham paid tithe to him

The Bible now says that Jesus Christ is a priest forever after the order (pattern, mandate, direction) of Melchizedek which means that for us as Christ followers, kingdom ambassadors and possessors of the license to succeed our actions must be after the order of Jesus Christ.

If Abraham paid tithe to Melchizedek, we must also pay tithe to Jesus. When we pay tithe, it is Jesus that receives it in heaven.

> Furthermore, here [in the Levitical priesthood] tithes are received by men who are subject to death; while there [in the case of Melchizedek], they are received by one of whom

it is testified that he lives [perpetually]. (Hebrews 7:8, TAB; Classic)

Another instruction, though controversial, says the following: "**I hate divorce**," says the God of Israel. God-of-the-angel-armies says, "I hate the violent dismembering of the 'one flesh' of marriage." So watch yourselves. Don't let your guard down. "Don't cheat" (Mal. 2:16, TAB).

It is extremely important that I mention the following regarding the above very touchy instruction. I hold no grudge neither do I condemn anybody who has been divorced, is in the process, or is considering it. When you hear of some people's situation and what transpired in their homes, you wonder in utter amazement, how could this wife or husband do such a heinous act? But the only true judge is the only wise God.

While I empathize with anybody who has been involved in divorce or is undergoing serious challenges in their marriage with its complexities, I am just reiterating kingdom instruction, not my own religious rites. I sincerely pray God's healing power will touch those homes and hearts in serious peril of divorce in Jesus's name, amen.

After having said the above, it is an unmistakable truth that the King hates divorce in His kingdom. According to kingdom constitution on marriage,

> For this reason, a man shall leave his father and his mother and shall be joined to his wife, and the two shall become one flesh. (Eph. 5:31, TAB)

When a man and a woman come together and say, "I do" in holy matrimony, there is a spiritual surgery that takes place in the heavenly kingdom, thereby joining the two into one. This is why the part of the ceremony that has to do with vow taking is called the "joining." Heaven joins the couple together. This is a mystery that is even more profound when there is a consummation of the holy matrimony.

> There's more to sex than mere skin on skin. Sex is as much spiritual mystery as physical fact. As written in Scripture, "The two become one. (1 Cor. 6:16, MSG)

When for any reason either of the couple or both of them decide to annul the covenant, it is not only a question of hiring an attorney or going before a

Justice of the Peace (what an irony) to dissolve the marriage, but there is also a surgery being placed on heaven to perform. This is referred to in kingdom constitution as a "violent dismembering of the 'one flesh' of marriage" (Mal. 2:16, MSG).

The question that crosses the mind is, "How could God, who performed such an intricate surgery of joining a couple to become one, now undertake a violent dismembering of the one flesh of marriage?"

My thought on this is that if there is a dismembering, it means the once-married couple who has now been divorced could be walking around with some degree of handicap. While the act of marriage is a spiritual surgery that is divinely crafted to produce one person, the divorce is a violent dismembering—just like how an accident happens and a limb is crushed. Imagine the pain. Such a person is disfigured and traumatized even though a prosthetic limb is given.

No matter how you look at it, there is a degree of pain associated with divorce for anybody that has been involved. Please think deeply and consider wisely. Sometimes we look at others most especially those that are highly placed in the kingdom that have divorced and they are still progressing. Based on this, we go ahead and separate from our husband or wife for even a flimsy reason. In the kingdom, we are not expected to look at other citizens as our example when they are not followers of the kingdom constitution but at the King through his word. It should be follow as Christ is being followed.

Above and beyond this, look at the response of the King to a question on divorce:

> Jesus replied, "Moses permitted divorce only as a concession to your hard hearts, but it was not what God had originally intended." (Matt. 19:8, TAB)

If divorce was not what God originally intended and Moses permitted it, it then means that if you are having challenges in your home make sure you abundantly seek the face of God before making any life altering decision. I sincerely pray that the Almighty God will guide and comfort you. Most importantly, before you enter into the marriage covenant, make sure God is the one that led you to your spouse. If he led you to your spouse, he will lead you through every storm. He is still the Prince of peace.

As clear instructions are present in our DNA for a meaningful and successful life, which represents what to do, so also is the blueprint.

Blueprint (How-to): A blueprint is an original plan or prototype that influences subsequent design or practice. Here is the blueprint of the Almighty God for humanity through Jesus Christ:

> But it was the LORD's good plan to crush him and fill him with grief. Yet when his life is made an offering for sin, he will have a multitude of children, many heirs. He will enjoy a long life, and the LORD's plan will prosper in his hands. When he sees all that is accomplished by his anguish, he will be satisfied. And because of what he has experienced, my righteous servant will make it possible for many to be counted righteous, for he will bear all their sins. I will give him the honors of one who is mighty and great, *because he exposed himself to death*. He was counted among those who were sinners. He bore the sins of many and interceded for sinners. (Isa. 53:10–12, NLT)

These three verses represent the death, burial, and resurrection of Jesus Christ. But the Bible calls this God's good plan or blueprint. How can God's good plan be the killing of his only begotten Son? It definitely portends that he knows something great that is beyond any human comprehension will be unveiled if he will only allow his only Son to die—the only Wise God indeed.

The Bible passage goes on to say that Jesus was highly exalted because he exposed himself to death (i.e., he allowed himself to be killed). The blueprint for us to fulfill our calling as the light of the world (our DNA), thereby utilizing our license for success effectively, is to "die."

> Listen carefully: Unless a grain of wheat is buried in the ground, dead to the world, it is never any more than a grain of wheat. But if it is buried, it sprouts and reproduces itself many times over. (John 12:24, MSG)

To die here does not mean that you should go and commit suicide but to mortify the deeds of the flesh. It is only a broken horse that becomes a thorough breed not a wild one. Your ability to obey the Word of God ensures that your flesh is no longer ruling. The fruit of the Spirit must become evident for all to see.

You could have the gifts of the Spirit, but they amount to nothing without the fruit. The fruit keeps the gifts flowing. Note the nuggets below:

- Allow yourself to be planted.
- To be planted involves being buried.
- Burial means death to the world and its fallacies but alive to the Word and the Truth.
- Recognize that this is a process.
- After correctly going through the process, there will be sprouting, harvesting, and reproduction.
- If there will be reproduction later on, it is advisable you plant what is good.
- It is what you plant that you will reap.

A major reason why God wants us to be planted is because of His wisdom. He knows anything that will endure must be firmly rooted so that a slight wind won't blow it away. This reveals the blueprint of how to excel in life. For any life to be outstanding, there must be a funeral service for everything that wants to stand in the way of success.

Myriads of activities always contest for our attention, but we must learn to choose that which is needful. You need to be dead to insults and accolades if you want to be somebody. Insults and accolades have killed many destinies, but when properly processed, they could be used as a stepping-stone to get out of the miry clay or to become outstanding.

Do Not Uproot the Seed

Without the seed, there can be no harvest. When the earth remains in seedtime, harvest shall not cease. You must be careful to protect the seed sown. The seed must not be corrupted.

> Being born again, not of corruptible seed, but of incorruptible, by the word of God, which liveth and abideth for ever. (1 Pet. 1:23, KJV)

Not uprooting the seed demonstrates you have faith in what God has said and what He is doing.

> For every good thing that God is doing that you cannot see, all you have to do is say Amen. For every hope that is still just a dream, it is by trusting in God that it will become a reality. (Bob Fitts)

Your faith in the promise of God will give you favor. Let the Word of God be mixed with faith in you so that it will profit you.

Let the Seed Die

As with any seed, for it to develop into fruit, it must be sown. The process of sowing involves accepting every jot of the Word. Our disposition should be "God has said it, I do believe it, I will then behave it to become it and that settles it."

> Forever O Lord your word is settled. (Ps. 119:89, NKJV)

At a time, King Jehoshaphat of Judah was preparing for war against three kings. He sought the face of God, and the response from the throne of grace was, "You will not have to fight in this battle, for the battle is not yours but the Lord's." He needed to convince the people so that the seed of victory will bear the fruit of victory.

> And they rose early in the morning, and went forth into the wilderness of Tekoa: and as they went forth, Jehoshaphat stood and said, Hear me, O Judah, and ye inhabitants of Jerusalem; Believe in the LORD your God, so shall ye be established; believe his prophets, so shall ye prosper. (2 Chron. 20:30, KJV)

Your establishment and prosperity from the words of prophecy paving the way to fulfill your destiny is dependent on allowing the seed to die.

Another keyword in the definition of DNA is **Structure.**

A structure is the mode of building, constructing, organizing, or arranging. Despite the fact that a builder possesses the blueprint, he still needs to build in such a way that what is being built will be structurally sound. In North

America, if you have been involved in the process of a new building, whether buying or constructing, you find that there is a stage in the construction process that is called a structural walk through.

This is an opportunity given to the owner of the building to make sure that whatever has been built so far is what the blueprint says. What a tragedy it would be to come and view a building that you have paid for only to discover the rooms and other structural parts are not what it is supposed to be. This is why the Bible says,

> According to the grace (the special endowment for my task) of God bestowed on me, like a skillful architect and master builder I laid [the] foundation, and now another [man] is building upon it. *But let each [man] be careful how he builds upon it,* For no other foundation can anyone lay than that which is [already] laid, which is Jesus Christ (the Messiah, the Anointed One). (1 Cor. 3:10–11, TAB)

Then the question could arise: how do you build or put structure(s) in place? Jesus Christ addressed this through a parable:

> Therefore, everyone who hears these words of mine and puts them into practice is like a wise man who built his house on the rock. The rain came down, the streams rose, and the winds blew and beat against that house; yet it did not fall, because it had its foundation on the rock. (Matt. 7:24–25, NIV)

You need to build according to the laid-down principles of the Word (i.e., you must not only be hearers but also doers). This attitude must be exemplified in your daily lives and attainment.

Paul the Apostle said, "Similarly, if anyone competes as an athlete, he does not receive the victor's crown unless he competes according to the rules" (2 Tim. 2:5, NIV).

This definitely means that you must know the Word of God to be able to lay down a good structure in all you do.

> How can a young person live a clean life? By carefully reading the map of your Word. I'm single-minded in pursuit

of you; don't let me miss the road signs you've posted. I've banked your promises in the vault of my heart so I won't sin myself bankrupt. (Ps. 119:9–11, MSG)

Let the following be your guide:

- He is the source; you depend on Him.
- Listen to Him.
- When He commands, you obey.
- You cannot choose to obey Him when it is convenient for you.
- If you detach yourself from Him, you have no life.
- If you are attached to Him, make sure it is a vital union (i.e., you cannot serve Him with your mouth, but your heart is far from Him).

Another very important keyword in the definition of DNA that must be present in the life of any person who is licensed to succeed is **Regulation (limits of what you can do):**

> GOD took the Man and set him down in the Garden of Eden to work the ground and keep it in order. GOD commanded the Man, "You can eat from any tree in the garden, except from the Tree-of-Knowledge-of-Good-and-Evil. Don't eat from it. The moment you eat from that tree, you're dead." (Gen. 2:15–17, MSG)

Regulation is a law, a rule, or an order prescribed by authority to direct conduct. It keeps you on course, and when you are on course, you last. We will deal with regulation in more detail in the chapter "Evolve"

No matter the height that you have attained, this next keyword is needed to remain relevant: **Development (your pattern of growth).**

> As soon as the meal was finished, he insisted that the disciples get in the boat and go on ahead to the other side while he dismissed the people. With the crowd dispersed, he climbed the mountain so he could be by himself and pray. He stayed there alone, late into the night. (Matt. 14:22–23, MSG)

Immediately, the crowd left Jesus in the above scripture. Jesus quickly told his disciples to leave that place, and he went to a solitary place to pray. He knew the only reason why the crowd always flocked to him was because they will always get a good "meal" to eat. He had to go to a place where he will get the recipe for another delicacy to keep the people coming.

In life, never forget this no matter the enterprise that you are involve in, anytime the "people" cannot get a "nutritious meal," they go and look for it someplace else.

Know this about life:

- People are always in search of a good meal. A meal here is the solution to the myriad of problems that mankind is engrossed in. This, therefore, means that, "If you have the desired meal, people will flock to your restaurant."
- There is always a meal to prepare. Irrespective of the breakthrough in the field of science or other human endeavor, there is always a great demand for more discoveries, whether in the field of medicine, engineering, or human kinetics.
- What sets any meal apart is the quality or culinary prowess of the chef.
- No matter the quantity of any meal, it can finish, or if not preserved, it will decay.
- Before a meal is finished, you need to start preparing another one.
- A meal is what you can eat or, in the broader sense, what you serve to others.
- A meal is the gift of God in you that is well put together in the right quantity, quality, and package.
- For any meal to be sought, it must be nutritious and balanced.
- What you serve to others could determine your relevance or self-worth.
- To prepare a good meal, you will need to be a skilled chef or partner with a skilled chef.
- Though there might be heat and discomfort in the kitchen when the meal is being prepared, ultimately there will be lofty heights of commendation and distinction.
- Make sure you have a garbage bin in your kitchen while preparing a meal to dispose unwanted ingredients.
- The place of solitude is the place of preparation.
- Solitude is a pathway to success.

Therefore, develop the gifts of God in you:

1. The place of His presence is where men are made. When the presence of God becomes amiable, you will create time to be there. "Come now and let us reason together" (Isa. 1:19a, TAB).

2. Decide to be part of God's inner circle. "Who is in the Lord's inner circle and sees and hears his word? Who pays attention and listens to his word?" (Jer. 23:18, GWT).

3. People who affect their generation have their occupation and preoccupation as God.

4. There is a place where eternal things are born and incubated, and it is in the presence of the Lord. "And as He was praying, the appearance of His countenance became altered (different), and His raiment became dazzling white [flashing with the brilliance of lightning]" (Luke 9:29, TAB).

5. Spending time with Him will "develop the picture."

It is not enough to obey instruction, follow the blueprint, have a structure, and develop. You must be **Functioning (be what you have been designed to be):**

> As long as I am in the world, I am the light of the world.
> (John 9:5, KJV)

When you know who you are, you will be able to do things that will augment the purpose for which you have been created. This prevents jealousy and allows you to appropriately "serve" the gift of God in your life.

Functioning according to your design showcases you as an original, not a copy. Do not be sorry for yourself; you are perfect for your purpose. You do not do things because it is the latest thing but because it is your eternal purpose.

At a time, John the Baptist was asked who he was.

> They asked him, "What then? Are you Elijah?" And he said, "I am not!" "Are you the Prophet?" And he answered, "No!" Then they said to him, "who are you? Tell us, so that we may

give an answer to those who sent us. What do you say about yourself?" *He said, "I am the voice of one crying aloud in the wilderness [the voice of one shouting in the desert]. Prepare the way of the Lord [level, straighten out, the path of the Lord],* as the prophet Isaiah said." (John 1:21–23, TAB)

Later on, the same people accosted Jesus and insinuated he was not crying in the wilderness, like John:

> For John came neither eating nor drinking, and they say, "He has a demon." The Son of Man came eating and drinking, and they say, "Here is a glutton and a drunkard, a friend of tax collectors and sinners." But wisdom is proved right by her deeds. (Matt. 11:18–19, TAB)

- Do not allow your design to be distorted and your functioning flawed.
- Don't allow people to confuse you.
- Nobody is born without a purpose.
- The joy of knowing your design is that you will not be intimidated by the success of others, you thereby leave the insignificants.
- Everything you have gone through in life is preparing you for your purpose—even your present affliction or crisis. "Many are the affliction of the righteous."
- For anything animate or inanimate that is formed to perform, though there is "storming", eventually there will be a "norming".

At this time, we have become a microwave generation. Always looking for the quick fix. You need to know that "when we travail, with diligence, we eventually triumph."

Every individual has a cross to carry.

> Sweet are the uses of adversity. (Shakespeare)

> Crisis in life is proof that everything you need to properly function is present but in the wrong location or quantity. You just need to reorder or reorganize.

Have you considered the situation in the beginning, when the earth was void and without form and darkness was upon the face of the earth, God just reordered everything?

In the book, "Leading Teams with Integrity" it is mentioned, "If there is a silver lining to bad times, it is this: when facing severe challenges, 'your mind normally is at its sharpest' "

Crisis is the incubator of creativity. There is no issue in life that cannot be solved.

Every problem in life has a name, and they are only awaiting the right command, voice, action, or influence. It is time for you to hit the right switch so that heaven will release the signal for your life of abundant success.

If you do all the above (instruction, blueprint, development, functioning) without this next one, no matter the height attained, it will just be temporal. You definitely need **Long-term storage (length of your stay with Him):**

> If you live in Me [abide vitally united to Me] and My words remain in you and continue to live in your hearts, ask whatever you will, and it shall be done for you. (John 15:7, TAB)

Continually, you need to live in Him. He is the only one who can continue to supply all your need.

When Jesus was on earth, He effectively operated according to His DNA, showing us how to be the light that we have been changed or translated to as citizens of the kingdom.

You need to operate according to your DNA so as to utilize your license to succeed.

3

Flourish

To flourish, you must understand that all the instructions laid down in the kingdom constitution (the Bible) is about the following:

1. *Redemption, not religion.* While religion imprisons, redemption empowers.

To empower means to give power or authority to somebody.

> But whoever did want him, who believed he was who he claimed and would do what he said, He made to be their true selves, their child-of-God selves. These are the God-begotten, not blood-begotten, not flesh-begotten, not sex-begotten. (John 1:12–13, MSG)

To empower means to enable or permit (i.e., the ability to do what one would not ordinarily or naturally be able to do).

When you become translated from the kingdom of darkness to that of light, you return to your true or child-of-God self. Where before you were an alien or strangers—illegal, foreigners to the commonwealth of spiritual Israel and her benefits—by being redeemed, you become familiar, legal, and citizens of the commonwealth. You have the license to succeed. All the benefits of the kingdom are now available to you.

Evaluate yourself to see if you reflect the characteristics of religion so that you can begin to make amends.

The following are the characteristics of religion:

- *Stagnant in perception.* It is always all about the letter devoid of compassion.

  Certainly, a human is more valuable than a sheep! So it is right to do good on the day of worship…The Pharisees left and plotted to kill Jesus. (Matt. 12:9–14, GWT)

- *Static in point.* A characteristic of those static in point is that anytime they see an individual, it is the stigma that the blood of Jesus has washed off that is still visible. Old things never pass away with such people. "The sin of Saul is still brought to bear on Paul." This could even manifest in an inability to forgive and move on even when apology has been rendered.

  The religion scholars and Pharisees led in a woman who had been caught in an act of adultery. They stood her in plain sight of everyone and said, "Teacher, this woman was caught red-handed in the act of adultery. Moses, in the Law, gives orders to stone such persons. What do you say?" They were trying to trap him into saying something incriminating so they could bring charges against him. Jesus bent down and wrote with his finger in the dirt. They kept at him, badgering him. He straightened up and said, "The sinless one among you, go first: Throw the stone." Bending down again, he wrote some more in the dirt. Hearing that, they walked away, one after another, beginning with the oldest. The woman was left alone. Jesus stood up and spoke to her. "Woman, where are they? Does no one condemn you?" "No one, Master." "Neither do I," said Jesus. "Go on your way. From now on, don't sin." (John 8:3–11, MSG)

- *Stuck in the past.* The same old way of thinking, behaving, and acting.

  Paul stood in the middle of the court and said, "Men of Athens, I see that you are very religious…In fact he is never far from any one of us…God overlooked the times when people didn't know any better. But now he commands everyone everywhere to turn to him and *change the way they think and act*." (Heb. 10:11; 27b; 30, GWT)

Peter needed to change the way he thought and acted:

"Get up Peter! Kill these animals, and eat them." Peter answered, "I can't do that, Lord! I've never eaten anything that is impure or unclean…Don't say that the things which God has made clean are impure." (Acts 10:13–15, GWT)

❖ *Suspicious of people.*

How can a Jewish man like you ask a Samaritan woman like me for a drink of water?…At that time his disciples returned. They were surprised that he was talking to a woman. *But none of them asked him, "What do you want from her?" or, "Why are you talking to her?"* (John 4:9, 27, GWT)

A pastor with dark pigmentation was once on a plane. A Caucasian woman looked at him and then walked to his seat and sat by him. Immediately, the pastor thought she was prejudiced, but for the duration of the flight from Houston to Toronto, this woman chatted with him. This erased his misconception and taught him a lesson: never prejudge, jump to a hasty conclusion, or categorize anybody based on a general opinion. You never can tell who is next to you or who will walk by you.

Redemption: a new and living way. This is a unique mystery that makes it difficult for the wise to accept Him—the simplicity and generosity. How can somebody who has never met you not only die for you but also leave for you an unending inheritance? This is why redemption is so huge; you have never seen him in person, but He knows you.

For those who understand this mystery, misery is taken from their lives, and they are conferred with mastery.

Known unto God are all his works from the beginning of the world. (Acts 15:18, KJV)

The following are characteristics of the redeemed:

❖ *Arrestable or "Apprehend-able"*

This takes total surrender. One of the reasons why some people find it challenging to do the will or bidding or obey the instructions of God is because they have not been arrested or apprehended.

> Not as though I had already attained, either were already perfect: but I follow after, if that I may apprehend that for which also I am apprehended of Christ Jesus. (Phil. 3:12, KJV)

Such people need to examine their salvation and check their license.

> Whoever is a believer in Christ is a new creation. The old way of living has disappeared. A new way of living has come into existence. (2 Cor. 5:17, GWT)

To understand the concept of *arrested* or *apprehended*, you have to look at those incarcerated. Most of their decision-making ability is taken away from them. They follow the rules and regulations that govern the running of the prison.

It is because Jesus Christ our Lord and Savior was apprehended that He could say,

> I have never spoken on My own authority or of My own accord or as self-appointed, but the Father Who sent Me has Himself given Me orders [concerning] what to say and what to tell. And I know that His commandment is (means) eternal life. So whatever I speak, I am saying [exactly] what My Father has told Me to say and in accordance with His instructions. (John 12:49–50, TAB)

For any man or woman that has been apprehended for the things of God, irrespective of your educational qualification, the things of God are not only appealing but also attainable. You are not only hearers but also doers.

> Although I could have confidence in my physical qualifications. If anyone else thinks that he can trust in something physical, I can claim even more. I was

> circumcised on the eighth day. I'm a descendant of Israel. I'm from the tribe of Benjamin. I'm a pure blooded Hebrew. When it comes to living up to standards, I was a Pharisee. When it comes to being enthusiastic, I was a persecutor of the church. When it comes to winning God's approval by keeping Jewish laws, I was perfect. These things that I once considered valuable; I now consider worthless for Christ. (Phil. 3:4–7, GWT)

What a complete turnaround!

- ❖ *Adaptable.* Instead of allowing insults to destroy you, use them to illuminate your life so that you can become distinct.

> I know how to be abased and live humbly in straitened circumstances, and I know also how to enjoy plenty and live in abundance. I have learned in any and all circumstances the secret of facing every situation, whether well-fed or going hungry, having a sufficiency and enough to spare or going without and being in want. (Phil. 4:12, TAB)

The woman with the issue of blood used what she had to get what she needed.

Develop the ability to turn crisis into a classroom. Adaptation is a virtue that all those that are redeemed must develop. Adaptation is the path to advancement.

> Before a young woman's turn came to go in to King Xerxes, she had to complete twelve months of beauty treatments prescribed for the women, six months with oil of myrrh and six with perfumes and cosmetics. (Esther 2:12, NIV)

Esther adapted to twelve months of immersion in oil so as to be enthroned as queen.

- ❖ *Advance-able.* Submission despite seeming superiority in knowledge, wealth, and other things to another.

Jesus said to her, "Why did you come to me? My time has not yet come…Jesus told the servers, "Fill the jars with water." (John 2:4; 7, GWT)

Examples of some people who received advancement due to submission are the following:

- *Elijah and Elisha.* Elisha submitted completely to Elijah.

   Here is Elisha the son of Shaphat, which poured water on the hands of Elijah. (2 Kings 3:11b, KJV)

   Elisha by reason of submission, received a wonderful benefit from Elijah—a blank cheque before Elijah left the earth.

   What should I do for you before I'm taken from you. (2 Kings 2:9b, GWT)

- *Naomi and Ruth.* Ruth forsook all and followed Naomi.

   Ruth who was from Moab, said to Naomi, "Please let me go to the field of anyone who will be kind to me. There I will gather the grain left behind by the reapers." Naomi told her, "Go my daughter." (Ruth 2:2, GWT)

   Naomi, Ruth's mother-in-law, said to her, "My daughter, shouldn't I try to look for a home that would be good for you?" (Ruth 3:1, GWT)

- *Almighty God the Father and Jesus.* Jesus surrendered to humiliation and a shameful death.

   Although he was in the form of God and equal with God, *he did not take advantage of this equality.* Instead he *emptied* himself by taking on the form of a servant…He *humbled* himself by becoming *obedient* to the point of death, death on a cross. This is why God has given him an exceptional honor. (Phil. 2:6–9a, GWT)

Advanceable does not only mean submission but also being resolute or determined (When you know according to the Word of God that submission is part of you, your countenance, and your actions, then you need to apply another principle for advancement. This is "gear force."

> From the time of John the Baptizer until now, the kingdom of heaven has been forcefully advancing. (Matt. 11:12a, GWT)

- ❖ *Achievable.* Knowing that His strength is made perfect in your weakness.

The super of God + the natural of man = Supernatural.

> I have strength for all things in Christ Who empowers me [I am ready for anything and equal to anything through Him Who infuses inner strength into me; I am self-sufficient in Christ's sufficiency]. (Phil. 4:13, TAB)

2. *Renewal, not recession.* Renewal demands a new way of thinking with an open mind to the possibilities of God, not the seeming impossibility of any situation.

> My son, listen, be wise, and keep your mind going in the right direction. (Prov. 23:19, GWT)

> Don't copy the behavior and customs of this world, but let God transform you into a new person by changing the way you think. Then you will learn to know God's will for you, which is good and pleasing and perfect. (Rom. 12:2, NLT)

What Is Recession?

It is a temporary depression in economic activity or prosperity. It is important to note the word *temporary*. The depression as a result of a recession is not permanent. This tells me we should not interact or respond to recession as if it is a permanent situation.

> For surely there is a latter end [a future and a reward], and your hope and expectation shall not be cut off. (Prov. 23:18, TAB)

Your disposition to the Word of God will determine your distinction in the sight of men and challenges. Look at how the kingdom handbook describes challenging situations: "light, momentary affliction (this slight distress of the passing hour)."

> So we're not giving up. How could we! Even though on the outside it often looks like things are falling apart on us, on the inside, where God is making new life, not a day goes by without his unfolding grace. These hard times are small potatoes compared to the coming good times, the lavish celebration prepared for us. (2 Cor. 4:16–17, MSG)

The following are the characteristics of recession:

- ❖ *Depression by falsehood.*

> But soon word was going around in Judah, The builders are pooped, the rubbish piles up; We're in over our heads, we can't build this wall. (Neh. 4:10, MSG)

> The origin of the complaint, accusation or insult determines the magnitude of the hurt.

Before the above depressing remarks, there had been several others, such as the following:

> What does this bunch of feeble jews think they are doing…
> Look at those charred stones they are pulling out of the rubbish and using again…That stone wall would collapse if even a fox walked along the top of it. (Neh. 4:2–3, NLT)

But insult now came from an unexpected source—Judah. Judah, who was supposed to not only be an encourager but also use praise as a protocol to access the throne of grace, had now joined the bandwagon.

Do not allow the depressing falsehood of men bring about a recession in your vision, thereby preventing your light from shining. Instead, pull out the charred stones from what is called rubbish and use it again.

Do not discard the charred stones. The stone the builders reject has a way of eventually becoming the cornerstone.

- ❖ *Regression by family.*

    Well-meaning family members can be your worst enemies. (Matt. 10:36, MSG)

As a family, most especially husbands and wives, you need to be careful of what you say to each other, most especially in times of adversity. Yours should not be, "Curse God and die."

Do not kill each other with the words of your mouth. Majority of people have a naturally active and defensive nature. This means that if somebody says something you perceive as insulting against you, the natural tendency is to react in like manner.

The depth of your negative reaction could be the demise and eventual decay of your family.

> The tongue is a small thing, but what enormous damage it can do. A tiny spark can set a great forest on fire. And the tongue is a flame of fire. It is full of wickedness that can ruin your whole life. It can turn the entire course of your life into a blazing flame of destruction. (James 3:5–6, NLT)

A question that you need to answer is, "Who is in your family?" (i.e., your network or immediate sphere of influence).

- ❖ *Oppression by fear.*

    What I always feared has happened to me. What I dreaded has come true. (Job 3:25, NLT)

Fear has been defined as "*f*alse *e*xpectation *a*ppearing *r*eal." Therefore, if the Bible says that the expectation of the righteous shall happen, then you have to be careful of what you are thinking of or expecting.

For as he thinks in his heart, so is he. (Prov. 23:7a, TAB)

A major input of recession economically is that it curtails the ability of people to buy and sell, thereby grinding the economy to a halt. This is always fuelled by fear. The fear of what will happen to the little that one has, "What if I lose my job?" what-ifs. The next recourse is to can all you have and sit on the can. The danger here is that you are not trading or buying because of fear. You use faith to buy what you need, but here, faith is thrown out of the door.

You can be in the midst of plenty but operating in recession when the mind-set of canning all you can envelopes you.

Renewal—a new way of thinking that resuscitates faith—faith is legal tender. You use it to purchase what you want. In the time of recession, what any true child of God must never stop doing is stop spending—spending their faith.

At a time of crisis or recession in the beginning, the creative ability of God was intact. Fear will take away your creative ability by not allowing you to exercise faith.

The Chinese use two brushstrokes to write the word *crisis*. One brushstroke stands for danger, the other for opportunity.

> In a crisis, be aware of the danger—but recognize the opportunity. (John F. Kennedy)

Jesus Christ said,

> The Kingdom of Heaven is like a mustard seed planted in a field. It is the smallest of all seeds, but it becomes the largest of garden plants; it grows into a tree, and birds come and make nests in its branches. (Matt. 12:31–32, NLT)

All that Jesus does in times of recession or challenges is plant a seed of faith—when there was no food, he asked one of his disciples where can we get food; to pay tax, he told Peter to go and fish; for people who needed healing, he says, "Do you have faith?"

Jesus spends the currency of faith through the avenue of a new way of thinking because He knows that in the spiritual, faith is legal tender—an acceptable means of transacting business or buying and selling.

In the world of real estate, the wise actually made millions in the time of the crisis of 2009. What others did not want the wise bought to now sell later at an exorbitant profit. It is the same concept in the spiritual. People stop operating according to spiritual principles in the time of recession. They gravitate toward worldly principles. They stop spending faith.

This grinds the flow of blessing to a halt because there is no activity in the spiritual realm for such people. This makes treasures abundantly available and easily accessible for those who are willing to do what it takes to spend their faith. When you spend faith, you are actually investing. You are sowing seeds into your account that you can withdraw from at a later date.

Here are the characteristics of renewal or of the renewed mind:

❖   *Myth breakers.*

Though the Bible says, "The first shall be the last," it does not mean the first has to be last always. Tremendous good can still come from you. The sour grapes that your parents or generations before you have eaten must not set your teeth on edge. The hand that was crossed in the physical can be uncrossed in the spiritual by your positive actions.

> But his father refused. "I know what I'm doing, my son," he said. "Manasseh, too, will become a great people, but his younger brother [Ephraim] will become even greater. His descendants will become a multitude of nations!" (Gen. 48:19, NLT)

For a time, Ephraim seemed to be winning, but Manasseh eventually broke that myth.

> "And I heard how many were marked with the seal of God. There were 144,000 who were sealed from all the tribes of Israel: from Manasseh…12,000. " (Rev. 7:4, 6, NLT)

❖   *Destiny shapers.*

The happenings of the past never prevent such people from possessing their possession. They believe that with God nothing shall be impossible.

> Nathanael answered him, "[Nazareth!] Can anything good come out of Nazareth?" Philip replied, "Come and see!" (John 1:46, TAB)

❖   *Poverty turners or wealth makers.*

Believe that what you have gone through is a necessary occurrence in your resume of life that will work for your good in your quest to attain a new dimension in kingdom living.

> The Fish Gate was built by the sons of Hassenaah. They laid the beams, set up its doors, and installed its bolts and bars. (Neh. 3:3, NLT)

Fish is a symbol of prosperity. This means the sons of Hassenaah built the gate of prosperity. Hassenaah means "thorny" or "been through hardship." The hardship you have gone through is a wonderful experience as you begin to build your fish gate because the past is a prologue. The past has a way of coming in handy.

When the sons of Hassenaah built the fish gate, it was properly built because of their past experience. There was a door, a beam, bolts, and bars. This means when the poverty turns into prosperity, it will remain. It will not grow wings and fly away.

- ❖ *Pathfinders.*

There is always a way no matter the obstacle or how vast the wilderness is.

> David said, "The Lord Who delivered me out of the paw of the lion and out of the paw of the bear, He will deliver me out of the hand of this Philistine." (1 Sam. 17:37, TAB)

> David replied to the Philistine, "You come to me with sword, spear, and javelin, but I come to you in the name of the LORD of Heaven's Armies—the God of the armies of Israel, whom you have defied. Today the LORD will conquer you, and I will kill you and cut off your head. And then I will give the dead bodies of your men to the birds and wild animals, and the whole world will know that there is a God in Israel!" (1 Sam. 17:45–46, NLT)

3. *"Reflecters", not "reflexers".* Your being a Christian does not automatically mean you possess wisdom, therefore, get wisdom.

Here are the characteristics of reflexers:

- ❖ *Act before they think.*

You must know how to engage your mind before your muscles. Your brain will always give you much more than your brawn can give you. Even in physical activities, your cerebral acumen is of great importance. What separates the great sportsmen from the mediocre is their ability to engage their brain. They think before they act.

> And the men of Israel were distressed that day, for Saul had placed the people under oath, saying, "Cursed *is* the man who eats *any* food until evening, before I have taken vengeance on my enemies." So none of the people tasted food…But Jonathan said, "My father has troubled the land. Look now, how my countenance has brightened because I tasted a little of this honey. How much better if the people had eaten freely today of the spoil of their enemies which they found! For now would there not have been a much greater slaughter among the Philistines?" (1 Sam. 14:25, 29–30, NKJV)

❖ *Leap before they look.*

It is not every open door that you walk through.

> In her letters she commanded: "Call the citizens together for fasting and prayer and give Naboth a place of honor." (1 Kings 21:9, NLT)

Ahab in the story is a type of unbeliever or weakness or indecision, Jezebel represents evil and all demonic apparatus while Naboth is a type with the license to succeed who does not know who he or she is. Naboth was told to undertake a fast, and because they said that he should be one of the resources in the order of program—"lead prayers" and he was also given a place of honour, he said, "Wow, after all these days I have been noticed." He never asked for the theme of the program, what he was supposed to pray for, what the order of the program was, and how long the prayer was.

If he had asked for the order of the program, he would have known the duties of those two rascals or scoundrels beside him. Their duty was to accuse him.

❖ *Shoot before they aim.*

You cannot always be shooting from the hips. If you have nothing to say, keep quiet. Silence is golden and it cannot be misquoted. You should not speak to hear your own voice. Weigh your words. Speak to make sense.

> Jephthah made a vow to the Lord and said, "If You will indeed give the Ammonites into my hand, then whatever comes out of the doors of my house to meet me when I return in peace from the Ammonites, it shall be the Lord's, and I will offer it up as a burnt offering"…Then Jephthah came to his house at Mizpah, and this is what he saw: his daughter coming out to meet him with tambourines and with dancing. And she was his only child; except for her he had no son or daughter. And when he saw her, he tore his clothes [in grief] and said, "Alas, my daughter! You have brought me great disaster, and you are the cause of ruin to me; for I have [a]made a vow to the Lord, and I cannot take it back." (Judges 11:30–31, 34–35, TAB)

❖ *Fly without landing gear.*

It is not enough to know how to fly. You also need to take care of how to land, else you crash. On a return flight, you take care of not only departure but also arrival. It is not every counsel that you should take. What the Lord says is more superior to what the angel of the Lord says. Have a discerning spirit.

> When the Lord spoke to me, he told me not to eat or drink there or go back on the road I took to get there. The old prophet said, "I'm also a prophet, like you. An angel spoke the Lord's word to me. He said, 'Bring him home with you so that he may have something to eat and drink.'" (But the old prophet was lying.) The man of God went back with him and ate and drank in his home.
>
> When they were sitting at the table, the Lord spoke his word to the old prophet who had brought back the man of God. The Lord also called to the man of God. He said, "This is

what the Lord says: You rebelled against the words from the Lord's mouth and didn't obey the command that the Lord your God gave you. You came back, ate, and drank at this place about which he told you, 'Don't eat or drink there.' That is why your dead body will not be allowed to be placed in the tomb of your ancestors." (1 Kings 13:17–22, GWT)

Here are the characteristics of reflectors:

❖ *Mind over muscle.*

Life is practical and not mystical. A mystical approach will always produce a miserable end. No one succeeds without engaging the use of the brain. When your mind is sound, faith becomes resounding.

> Then the woman came back to Jesus, went to her knees, and begged. "Master, help me." He said, "It's not right to take bread out of children's mouths and throw it to dogs." She was quick: "You're right, Master, but beggar dogs do get scraps from the master's table." Jesus gave in. "Oh, woman, your faith is something else. What you want is what you get!" Right then her daughter became well. (Matt. 15:25–28, MSG)

❖ *Patience over panic.*

Your patience in the time of crisis will always channel a path to conquest. One thought that must never leave you in moments of difficulties is that God has already made a way—you just need to locate it.

> The religion scholars and Pharisees led in a woman who had been caught in an act of adultery. They stood her in plain sight of everyone and said, "Teacher, this woman was caught red-handed in the act of adultery. Moses, in the Law, gives orders to stone such persons. What do you say?" They were trying to trap him into saying something incriminating so they could bring charges against him.
>
> Jesus bent down and wrote with his finger in the dirt. They kept at him, badgering him. He straightened up and said,

"The sinless one among you, go first: Throw the stone." Bending down again, he wrote some more in the dirt.

Hearing that, they walked away, one after another, beginning with the oldest. The woman was left alone. Jesus stood up and spoke to her. "Woman, where are they? Does no one condemn you?" "No one, Master." "Neither do I," said Jesus. "Go on your way. From now on, don't sin." (John 8:3–11, MSG)

❖ *Wisdom, not worry.*

The worry about tomorrow will sap you of the strength for today. When you get into the worrying mode, you are not able to engage the intellect to make any informed decision. Worrying puts you on the treadmill of errors. You become error prone and start living in the dungeon of regrets. Engage wisdom, and all your detractors are silenced.

Then Jesus went into the temple courtyard and began to teach. The chief priests and the leaders of the people came to him. They asked, "What gives you the right to do these things? Who told you that you could do this?" Jesus answered them, "I, too, have a question for you. If you answer it for me, I'll tell you why I have the right to do these things. Did John's right to baptize come from heaven or from humans?"

They discussed this among themselves. They said, "If we say, 'from heaven,' he will ask us, 'Then why didn't you believe him?' But if we say, 'from humans,' we're afraid of what the crowd might do. All those people think of John as a prophet." So they answered Jesus, "We don't know." Jesus told them, "Then I won't tell you why I have the right to do these things." (Matt. 21:23–27, GWT)

4

Evolve

An interesting fact in the book of beginning is the shapelessness and emptiness that was the earth then.

> IN THE beginning God (prepared, formed, fashioned, and) created the heavens and the earth. The earth was without form and an empty waste, and darkness was upon the face of the very great deep. (Gen. 1:1–2, TAB)

Earth was full of darkness, but the transforming power of God brought shape, fullness, and light to earth. What readily came to my mind when reading this account is that God can create something from nothing and somebody from a nobody.

When you look at your life, this should give you joy because I know that no matter how terrible your situation or life might seem, there can be a transformation. In the book of Genesis, you see certain principles God applied in bringing about a transformation. This will reveal how to bring transformation to any unsightly situation that you encounter.

The word *transformation* means to undergo a change in form, appearance, character, or condition. God, who brought about a change to what looks like a useless condition, will bring a change to that situation of yours that has made you depressed and restless.

Another thing that brings me great joy when looking at Genesis 1:1–2 is that in the sight of God, no situation is useless. Even in the dunghill of life, God can decorate you. You may look at your situation and conclude that there is no hope, but he is the hope of the hopeless. Any change or transformation that you desire is inherent in that situation. The intervention needed on man's and God's part is to accelerate the change.

Transformation can be positive, but it can also be negative. A negative transformation is when something or someone goes from grace to grass, prosperity to poverty, and righteousness to sin. I will concentrate more on the positive transformation—how you can achieve the positive change that you desire.

Paul the Apostle advised, "Be transformed by the renewing of your mind." The mind has an important role to play in transformation. Man has a tendency to conform to the external superficial customs of the world. When we encounter an adverse situation, the first thing that comes to many people's mind is a way out, but more often than not, the solution we come up with are mostly quick fixes, not lasting solutions.

Sometimes, the solutions are crooked, even for Christians. It takes a measure of discipline or restraint to be able to go to the Word and to the Godly solution. We take the shape of the environment we find ourselves in and also reason according to the popular norm.

A case in point is King Saul. His concern was what people would think about him when Samuel told him that God already rejected him as king (1 Samuel 15:24-31). The challenge with taking the shape of the environment is that we limit ourselves. Water poured into a bottle has limited capability compared to that in a river or ocean.

Man, as in human, is vain and wants to be identified or recognized because of this. Man follows the ideas of the environment he is in and forgets the ideals. If God had followed the ideas of the earth in the beginning, there would not have been a change into what we have now. Paul the Apostle in the book of Romans 12:2 is advising us to embrace God's ideals.

The question now is, what are God's ideals? To discover God's ideals for transformation, we need to go back to the book of Genesis.

> IN THE beginning God (prepared, formed, fashioned, and) created the heavens and the earth. The earth was without form and an empty waste, and darkness was upon the face of the very great deep. The Spirit of God was moving

(hovering, brooding) over the face of the waters. And God said, Let there be light; and there was light. And God saw that the light was good (suitable, pleasant) and He approved it; and God separated the light from the darkness. (Gen. 1:1–4, TAB)

From the above passage we get the principles of transformation. This demonstrates how you can evolve to whom God has ordained you to be irrespective of the situation that you are facing. It is given in life that you will always face one thing or the other, but you must know how to deal with them for a life of victory always.

The Principles of Transformation

Begin

You cannot be in situ and expect transformation. No matter how good the plan is on paper, it is in execution that it will be proven. Everything in life has a beginning. A beginning is the start. The ability to start is absent in a lot of people. Instead of beginning, a whole lot of people have been bemoaning or procrastinating.

Beginning implies birth, and with birth comes visibility and noise (e.g., a baby).

Due to the fact that many people are not sure of the growth progression of what they will birth, they do not want to begin. A baby is not expected to behave like an adult when born. The baby will be fed and cleaned. A baby will not ask to go to the washroom when he or she is about to poo or pee. Many people run away from such challenges and do not want to give birth.

The good thing is that there is encouragement from the Word of God for those who are afraid of taking a positive step.

> And though your beginning was small, yet your latter end would greatly increase. (Job 8:7, TAB)

Another verse of the scripture says,

> Then another message came to me from the LORD: "Zerubbabel is the one who laid the foundation of this Temple, and he will complete it. Then you will know that the LORD of Heaven's Armies has sent me. Do not despise these small beginnings, *for the Lord rejoices to see the work begin,* to see the plumb line in Zerubbabel's hand. (Zech. 4:8–10, NLT)

To begin implies that something is about to evolve. You are laying a foundation. If you do not lay a foundation, you cannot complete a building. Based on the Word of God, when you begin, there are two atmospheres that you create: heaven and earth, dominant and recessive, and invisible to visible.

Heaven represents the successful finished picture of what you plan to achieve or the transformation that you desire while the earth represents what you have. The journey of transformation involves making earth look like heaven.

> So He said to them, "When you pray, say: Our Father in heaven, Hallowed be Your name. Your kingdom come. Your will be done on earth as it is in heaven." (Luke 11:2, NKJV)

This is one of the reasons why psychologists, psychotherapists, and motivational speakers encourage you to have a picture of the change that you desire pasted all around your room. What this does is that it helps to bring your mind to where you are going when situations that you see cause your mind to deviate from the charted path.

I was watching an investigative report on CNN regarding rehabilitation for amputees, and a form of therapy enunciated is what is called a mirror image. A mirror is placed facing the good limb, and because it is a mirror image, it creates the impression that the other leg is available. The amputee looks at this image and processes it in his mind that he or she still has a leg. Despite the fact that in reality the leg is amputated, in his mind, he pictures a leg. This helps in dealing with everyday life.

Though the earth was void and formless at a point, there was a beginning that led to change. There is always a force (seen or unseen) that sets something or someone in motion. As an individual, if you want to be somebody relevant in life, you have to start from somewhere.

As an organization, if you want to be a relevant conglomerate, know it will not happen by standing still. The dynamism of the evolving technology must be embraced.

As a church, if you want to move to a facility that will accommodate your ministry needs, you need to do something together to realize that dream. The pastor needs to not only pray but also lead in giving. The financial statement of the church must be well packaged, and the realtors must be diligent in searching for a suitable place.

There is no promise of God in the scripture that does not demand action.

> Rise up, take your journey, and pass over the Valley of the Arnon. Behold, I have given into your hand Sihon the Amorite, king of Heshbon, and his land; begin to possess it and contend with him in battle. This day will I begin to put the dread and fear of you upon the peoples who are under the whole heavens, who shall hear the report of you and shall tremble and be in anguish because of you. (Deut. 2:24–25, TAB)

Life does not give you what you deserve or dream but what you decide and do.

Despite the fact that God told the Israelites that He has given them the land, he still said they should "rise up" and "begin to possess it." Begin to make plans for the new job, children, marriage, landed immigrant papers, or prosperity that you desire.

Believe

It is an honorable thing to begin; however, the predecessor of *begin*, which serves as a lubricant to success, is *believe*.

Before you begin anything in life, whether positive or negative, there is a level of confidence or belief that what you are starting will succeed. An architect who designs a building has some level of confidence in his or her expertise to design a structure that will not only be built but also stand the test of time.

Hear this account about Jesus:

> When Jesus looked out and saw that a large crowd had arrived, he said to Philip, "Where can we buy bread to feed these people?" He said this to stretch Philip's faith. He already knew what he was going to do. (John 6:5–6, MSG)

"He already knew what He was going to do" meant He had a staunch belief in His ability to provide food for the multitudes. But at that time, Philip could not see it—it was formless.

You may have a picture of a glorious end to a project, but when you begin, it will be to some extent "formless and empty." This is a time that doubt will set in. A good example is somebody who is trying to abstain from food for a given period of time (midnight till 6:00 p.m.). Depending on the person's eating habits, if the individual normally eats breakfast at 8:00 a.m., the belly will give a grace of about an hour. By 9:00 a.m., the belly will complain, "Why are you treating me like this?" This message will also be relayed to the brain, and it may manifest in a form of dizziness or headache. The mind will pick up the code and declare, "You cannot do it. It is time for you to give in."

For those who have dealt with such before, you know that in less than thirty minutes after this crisis, all these symptoms will disappear (if you are not an ulcer patient). Everything is just a mind game. If you give in, you will start to regret, but if you did not, you will rejoice. The same thing applies in the journey of transformation.

> If you do not believe, you cannot receive. If you do not receive, you cannot become.

What is driving your belief is greater than any challenge that you might encounter. Before the Almighty spoke at all, "The Spirit of God was moving (hovering, brooding) over the face of the waters." It is important for you to realize, know, and believe that the spirit of God is always hovering and brooding over any adversity that you are facing to effect a transformation.

> And the power of the Lord was present to heal them. (Luke 5:17b, NKJV)

That statement was the belief that drove the sick man in the story and his friends to break down the roof.

Listen, there is always a roof over the power of God to transform you. You are responsible for breaking down the roof of doubt and other forms of limitation so that your desired transformation can be realized.

> You can't fly a kite unless you go against the wind and have a weight to keep it from turning a somersault. The same with man. No man will succeed unless he is ready to face and overcome difficulties and is prepared to assume responsibilities. (William J. H. Boetcker)

When Jesus was told about the sickness of Jairus's daughter, he could not come to his house immediately. He had to attend to the woman with the issue of blood. As He was going to the house of Jairus, He was given the news that the young girl had passed away:

> While He was still speaking, a man from the house of the director of the synagogue came and said [to Jairus], Your daughter is dead; do not weary and trouble the Teacher any further. (Luke 8:49, TAB)

The point at which the director of the synagogue found himself is the point where many wonderful projects meet their death. When it seems nothing good can come from an initiative, we quit.

> Unless a man has been kicked around a little, you can't really depend upon him to amount to anything. (William Feather)

The response of Jesus to Jairus was,

> Do not be seized with alarm or struck with fear; simply believe [in Me as able to do this], and she shall be made well. (Luke 8:50, TAB)

> Many men owe the grandeur of their lives to their tremendous difficulties. (Charles H. Spurgeon)

The difficulties we encounter want to do only one thing: seize our faith. "Do not let difficulties define you, define difficulties." You need to believe that as you have begun, you will succeed. God already knew there would be difficulties and challenges in life.

Do you know that as parents we are so full of worries about our children—what they are doing and what they are not doing? We compare them to everybody imaginable. Am I trying to say you should not be concerned about your children? Definitely no! All you have to do is know who they are:

> Don't you see that children are GOD's best gift? The fruit of the womb his generous legacy? Like a warrior's fistful of arrows are the children of a vigorous youth. Oh, how blessed are you parents, with your quivers full of children! Your enemies don't stand a chance against you; you'll sweep them right off your doorstep. (Ps. 127:3-5 MSG)

The first statement in the above verses is a question. Therefore, if your child is God's best gift and generous legacy, that child cannot turn to be a worst gift for God is not a wicked God. See your children through God's eyes. Eyes that see are few.

You need to know that the blessing of the Lord makes rich, and He does not add sorrow to it. I appeal to you to believe this. Make sure you "train" them in the way of the Lord.

When you do that, you have sown a seed into their life. The conclusion of the whole matter is that, "Your enemies don't stand a chance against you; you'll sweep them right off your doorstep." Whatever comes knocking on your door, you will eventually sweep them off your doorstep. It may be waywardness, sickness, rebellion, promiscuity, etc. The answer had already been settled; "you'll sweep them right off your doorstep" into the dustbin of forgetfulness in Jesus's name, amen.

As I was putting this together, the Spirit of God ministered to me that the main reason why parents even worry is not for the child but because of what people will say: "How can the son or daughter of —— behave this way?" What they seem to forget is that children who have been dedicated to the Lord and trained in the way of the Lord are His heritage. Therefore, they are children of God, and He is still able to care for His own.

Paul the Apostle declared,

> And this is why I am suffering as I do. Still I am not ashamed, for I know (perceive, have knowledge of, and am acquainted with) Him Whom I have believed (adhered to and trusted

in and relied on), and I am [positively] persuaded that He
is able to guard and keep that which has been entrusted to
me and which I have committed [to Him] until that day. (2
Tim. 1:12, TAB)

Paul, while in prison, made this declaration. He knew that though his physical body is in prison, the Word of God cannot be imprisoned. Hallelujah!

Belief helps you to have an imprint of your victorious end in your mind:

Fix this picture firmly in your mind: Jesus, descended from
the line of David, raised from the dead. It's what you've
heard from me all along. It's what I'm sitting in jail for right
now—but God's Word isn't in jail! (2 Tim. 2:8–9, MSG)

Let me try to explain something to you about belief. You remember I said that it must be there before and after you begin; what this tells you is that it is a pivot and not a foundation. While a foundation is what something rests on, a pivot does more than that. You do not only rest on a pivot but also use it to turn, rotate, or oscillate.

It can be described as something you depend on for vitality. While a foundation can be said to be passive, a pivot is active. Depending on your degree of belief, you can use a pivot to ascend or descend.

When Jehoshaphat and Judah were going to war without weapons but with worship, he had to assure the people:

and as they went out, Jehoshaphat stood and said, "Hear
me, O Judah, and you inhabitants of Jerusalem! Believe in
the Lord your God and you shall be established; believe and
remain steadfast to His prophets and you shall prosper." (2
Chron. 20:20, TAB)

Jesus Christ also used it as a pivot to make sure that His disciples firmly focus on Him:

Let not your heart be troubled; you believe in God, believe
also in Me. (John 14:1, NKJV)

Be Bold

> And God saw that the light was good. Then he separated the light from the darkness. God called the light "day" and the darkness "night." And evening passed and morning came, marking the first day. (Gen. 1:4–5, NLT)

Another important ingredient for transformation as you evolve into who God has called you to be is boldness. This means exhibiting courage and bravery. Sometimes, an individual who is bold could be daring, bordering on arrogance, but it must not tend towards stupidity.

At a time, a brother (Asahel) of Joab (a general of King David) ran after another general by the name Abner. The brother was asked to go back, but he did not, and he ended up dying shamelessly.

> Asahel refused to turn aside; so Abner with the rear end of his spear smote him through the abdomen, and he fell and died where he fell. And all who came to the place where Asahel fell and died stood still. (2 Sam. 2:23, TAB)

I know sometimes a man may need to die for what he believes in but ensure that what you believe in is right. When Abner looked back, he took the path of honor when he not only recognized Asahel to be the brother of a general but also, so as not to be shamefaced when others in Asahel's camp ask him what happened, Abner said he should instead slay one of the young men and take his sword as a trophy. Asahel was obstinate and adamant. He wanted the biggest trophy.

I want to take this opportunity as we begin to talk about boldness to emphasize that you have to make sure you are not being stubbornly stupid. Notice that before boldness, there was belief. You need to believe in the right thing. The Word of God says, "The wicked flee though no one pursues, but the righteous are as bold as a lion" (Prov. 28:1, TNIV).

At different ends of the spectrum are the righteous and the wicked. While the wicked will even run from their shadow, the righteous is bold. To be righteous means to be in right standing with God.

Before you start proclaiming boldness, make sure you are in right standing. Ensure that any stand you are taking on any matter does not contravene the

Word of God. You could be sincerely bold but sincerely wrong. What should drive boldness in any man or woman is wisdom.

> Who is as the wise man? And who knoweth the interpretation of a thing? A man's wisdom maketh his face to shine, and the boldness of his face shall be changed. (Ecclesiastes 8:1, KJV)

This passage talks about the value of right knowledge. Some people use a stern face to mask a lack of knowledge. They squeeze up their face, but in fact, they know nothing. This means it is not how wrinkly or rumpled up a face is that determines boldness. It is what you know that causes radiance and brightness.

> Joseph, he of Arimathea, noble and honorable in rank and a respected member of the council (Sanhedrin), who was himself waiting for the kingdom of God, daring the consequences, took courage and ventured to go to Pilate and asked for the body of Jesus. (Mark 15:43, TAB)

What enabled Joseph of Arimathea to take that risk is knowledge. The Word of God says he was waiting for the kingdom of God. Do not be bold in stupidity.

It was a bold move on the part of God that allowed Him to say, "Let there be light," knowing fully well that "He is able to call those things that be not as though they were." God then called the light day and the darkness night. This is a very important example for us as children of God—naming our situations and circumstances. Names, most especially good names, are like precious ointment. It is boldness that will make you to say this situation will only cause the name of God to be glorified.

I remember a story that was shared by the general overseer of the Redeemed Christian Church of God at a time when the mission had just built a new auditorium (at that time a small one). He inspected it, and everyone rejoiced. Shortly after, when the people came back, they saw the auditorium had been leveled not by the hands of men but of the weather.

The general overseer said that this was nothing but the devil at work. He then made a bold pronouncement that let us slap the devil by building a better one, and in record time also. They went all out and built a new and bigger one. He could have taken the route of mourning and crying over what had happened, but it would have led to more rejoicing in the pit of hell. Be bold and be strong, for the Lord your God is with you.

When you wake up, no matter how challenging it is, name the day. This is the day of mercy, goodness, favor, holiness, etc. This is the day that the Lord has made, I will rejoice and be glad in it. This is one of the reasons why we are in a season of overflow of His blessings. Your blessings shall overflow in Jesus's name. He shall prepare a table before you in the presence of your enemies, and your cup shall run over.

Look at this: "And evening passed and morning came, marking the first day" (Gen. 1:5, NLT).

The evening will pass. No matter how gloomy the situation is, it will pass away. In the Bible, you will always see, "And it came to pass" but not "And it came to stay." Whatever you are facing or going through will soon go into the sea of oblivion in Jesus's name. For weeping may endure for a night, but joy comes in the morning. You are stepping into that period of rejoicing called morning in Jesus's name.

Whatever you do not confront, you will not correct. Cowards die a thousand times before their death. Faith, they say, is risky business.

> So let us come boldly to the throne of our gracious God. There we will receive his mercy, and we will find grace to help us when we need it most. (Heb. 4:16, NLT)

How to exhibit boldness?

1. Do I have enough knowledge about the situation?

Before David went against Goliath, one of the important questions that he asked is, "What will be done for the man who kills this Philistine and removes this disgrace from Israel?" (1 Sam. 17:26a, NKJV). You need to know what you are entering into and the repercussions of your actions. We have an adage that goes, "If a young man is not well equipped, he should not ask for the kind of death that killed his father." This is to prevent him from also dying an untimely death from the hands of those who killed his father.

> Is there anyone here who, planning to build a new house, doesn't first sit down and figure the cost so you'll know if you can complete it? If you only get the foundation laid and

then run out of money, you're going to look pretty foolish. Everyone passing by will poke fun at you: 'He started something he couldn't finish. (Luke 14:28–30, MSG)

The knowledge you have about the cause of action you are about to embark upon will assist you in doing it right.

In many developing nations, most especially in the tropical regions of Africa, the chicken (hen and cock) graze in the open. They are not confined to the cage except at night. The chicks, seeing the parents going to graze, sometimes feel, "I can also do whatever they are doing."

What the chicks do not know is that the parents go out based on knowledge. They observe the environment and also look up into the sky. They look into the sky because they know that the eagle is lurking up above looking for a prey. The chicks, because of this lack of knowledge, feel the parents are being wicked when they are not allowed to go and graze, not realizing that they are just being prevented from an untimely death, most especially from the eagle.

An adage therefore says, "We are trying to prevent a chick from death, and it is saying they are not allowing me to go and graze."

Before you slap your wife—especially in a developed nation (abusing your spouse in any clime is wrong and is to be condemned)—know that those who did it before you have landed in jail. If you are doing it and you are getting away with it, it could be because your time to go to jail has not come. Husbands love your wife—not Internet pornography, your job, adultery, other women, or another man's wife.

For a wife, if you are cantankerous or troublesome and you are being told to take it easy and respect your husband but you keep on saying, "It is what is on my mind that I will do," all you have to do is check with others who have done it before you. They did what was on their mind, but eventually, they got what was not on their mind.

Immediately after 6 in the numerals there is 7, but then after 7, you still have 8, 9, 10, etc. Due to the fact that it is only 7 that is easily visible after 6 does not mean 7 is the end of the line. An adage says, "What is after 6 is more than 7." Be cautious so that you do not get what you did not bargain for.

> They charge like warriors; they scale walls like soldiers. They all march in line, not swerving from their course. They do not jostle each other; each marches straight ahead. They plunge through defenses without breaking ranks. (Joel 2:7–8, TNIV

1. Will the outcome glorify God or man?
2. What is my motive in embarking on this action?
3. What will be the repercussion or aftereffect of my action? For every action, there is a corresponding reaction both in the natural and the supernatural.

Boundary

> Then God said, "Let there be a space between the waters, to separate the waters of the heavens from the waters of the earth." And that is what happened. God made this space to separate the waters of the earth from the waters of the heavens. God called the space sky. (Gen. 1:6–8, NLT)

A boundary can be described as a limit or barrier of any kind. It is anything that restrains or obstructs. As humans, we are made up of boundaries physiologically. While our veins and arteries function as pathway for the flow of blood, they also double as boundaries to make sure the blood flows purposefully and not aimlessly.

When the barriers (blood vessels) are breached, it constitutes a serious problem (e.g., the rupturing of an artery in the brain called aneurysm leads to blood leak, or hemorrhaging). We have a brain, but it is contained in a barrier called the skull. Imagine if your brains are hanging out or your intestines are spilling over. Boundaries keep us from malfunctioning.

Boundaries are very important in life because they prevent a life of disorderliness. To ensure the world at that time was just not full of water, God made a separation to guarantee that we have a habitable place to live in.

For direction during a journey of transformation, you need boundaries.

After the creation of man, the first commandment ever given to man was a barrier or boundary:

> And the Lord God commanded the man, saying, You may freely eat of every tree of the garden; But of the tree of the knowledge of good and evil and blessing and calamity you shall not eat, for in the day that you eat of it you shall surely die. (Gen. 2:16–17, TAB)

To make sure Adam was focused and purposeful, he was told what was expected of him. When you cross boundaries that should guide you in life, the effect can be grave. Boundaries are things that ensure you are disciplined so that your future can be glorious:

> No discipline is enjoyable while it is happening—it's painful! But afterward there will be a peaceful harvest of right living for those who are trained in this way. (Heb. 12:11, NLT)

In life, there are always situations and things that want to prevent you from excelling or proving what is good, acceptable, and perfect in the will of God. You need to put a space between yourself and those things. Consider the fact that God could have let the waters of the heavens touch that of the earth, but he created a barrier, space, or firmament to separate the waters. This space God called sky.

From the sky, you have clouds, dew, rain, the moon, stars, etc. The fact that the sky is suspended does not mean it will not release the good treasures like rain, the moon, etc., within it. The same thing applies to you and me; the fact that you are told not to do something now does not mean when the time comes you won't be able to do it, or the benefits will still not come.

You need to shield yourself from anything that wants to exalt itself above the knowledge of God. It could be visible or invisible—invisible in the form of thoughts and imaginations and visible in the form of excessive spending, bad habits, disobedience, slothfulness, drunkenness, etc.

You may tell a man or woman to exercise caution in his or her spending habits. If the response is no, this negative action may show up when he or she is about to buy a property in the form of bad credit. The individual could then constitute a credit risk. When others are getting a prime interest rate, this individual's rate will be as if money is being borrowed from a loan shark or shylock.

> How well God must like you—you don't hang out at Sin Saloon, you don't slink along Dead-End Road, you don't go to Smart-Mouth College. Instead you thrill to God's Word, you chew on Scripture day and night. You're a tree replanted in Eden, bearing fresh fruit every month, Never dropping a leaf, always in blossom. (Ps. 1:1–3, MSG)

The first Psalm talks about benefits of not overstepping boundaries God has put in place. Do not hang out at Sin Saloon; instead, go to Bible Study and engage in meaningful activities to improve your status in life. Don't slink along Dead-End Road; instead, participate in duties that will promote life and godly living. Do not go to Smart-Mouth College; instead, think clearly before you speak.

Boundaries serve as a hedge around every child of God. "And whoso breaketh an hedge, a serpent shall bite him" (Eccles. 10:8, KJV).

Boundaries help you know when to spend and when to invest or save. No matter how much you earn, if you do not have boundaries, it may lead to poverty. There are always demands on money. Some people will tell you that even before they get paid their salary is gone. This is because all manners of needs—or in some cases, wants—are already lining up to take their share. It is up to you to determine the highly important from the pretenders.

> The slothful man roasteth not that which he took in hunting: but the substance of a diligent man is precious. (Prov. 12:27, NLT)

To roast implies refining, processing, and preservation. If you do not process and preserve inflow, you will not be able to regulate outflow. Unregulated outflow is a pathway to penury.

Boundaries assist us to be organized. It prevents a life of haphazard living. When you do not have boundaries, you are not able to plan your life properly.

Let me expand on an illustration that I once heard from Dr. Mensah Otabil about the life of Esau and Jacob.

Esau was the firstborn with the ability to carry all the blessings that should be for the firstborn. While he was a hunter, his brother, a stay-at-home man

(Gen. 25:27), always had something to cook. When Esau would go hunting, you wonder what he did with all the animals he hunted. He could have saved some. There are different ways of hunting: you can set a trap that will ensure you get the animal alive, or you can kill with a spear or arrow in those days.

If he chose the hunting technique of setting a trap, he could have a mini animal farm at home.

One thing that is evident is that he did not have an animal farm. This is because he was living for the moment. He was unable to preserve inflow that led to unregulated outflow. He always relied on his brother. "My brother will always have something cooked," he would think, not knowing that this so-called brother had a plan.

The plan came into manifestation one day when Esau came back from hunting, and I believe on this particular day, he caught nothing, and he told his brother.

> One day Jacob was cooking a stew. Esau came in from the field, starved. Esau said to Jacob, "Give me some of that red stew—I'm starved!" That's how he came to be called Edom (Red). (Gen. 25:30, MSG)

Do you realize that "Give me a little food" now may become "Sell me your birthright" later? When you do not have boundaries in life, you will trade away your future.

Do you know that because Esau could not plan—"The slothful man roasteth not that which he took in hunting: but the substance of a diligent man is precious" (Prov. 12:27, KJV)—when his father said, "Go and prepare food," he could have gone to his farm, killed a goat, or any other choice animal but he had none? Even if he had no live animal, he could have taken from those that he had preserved through roasting, but he also had none. He had to go hunting afresh.

What happens in life is that the continuous use of anything leads to depreciation except there is rest and refurbishment. It is the same forest he went to every time. The animals now understood his tactics better. There were now reduced animals. All the animals knew Esau was coming, and they fled to other areas. It was no coincidence he had to go through endless labor while his brother, who was not a hunter, experienced effortless triumph.

A question we can ask is, where did Jacob get the animal that he killed? It could probably be from Esau. Maybe he bought it from him. Boundaries show you off as a man of wisdom.

In life, there will always be tasks to do, but remember, there is only one individual. No matter how good you are at multitasking, one day, the body will complain. When the body begins to speak and you refuse to listen, instead of breaking through, the body might break down.

Boundaries prevent you from just living a life of copying. While there is nothing wrong in following an example already laid (make sure you do not infringe on copyright laws), you should, however, not make that your lifestyle. There has to be value added.

I clearly remember my final year in the university when I started following some of my friends to read in the lecture hall at night. Prior to this, I was used to reading in my room at night or going to the library in the daytime. From my room to the lecture hall was a distance of about two kilometers. We would chat endlessly before getting there, buy some snacks on the way, meet lots of friends in the lecture hall, and chat and gist some more before we finally settled down to read.

I found out that after reading for thirty minutes I was either falling asleep or resuming another bout of chatting. It suddenly dawned on me that I was setting myself up for failure. I tried to copy a style I was not used to and did not have enough time to adapt to. I quickly reverted to what I had tried, tested, and proven to be true and workable.

Boundaries bring about balance.

Why Do We Need Boundaries?

Here are some reasons why boundaries are necessary:

- *There is a path of life.* In life, there is a path that we all need to go through. Even for Jesus, there was Palm Sunday before Good Friday (John 12:13).
- *There is a process in life.* Transformation is a process. When you do not go through the right process, a fake product is produced. Mary had to spend time with Elizabeth for three months (Luke 1:39–56).

- *There is a plan for life.* We are assured and know that [God being a partner in their labor] all things work together and are [fitting into a plan] for good to and for those who love God and are called according to [His] design and purpose" (Rom. 8:28, AMP). There must be John the Baptizer before Jesus the Christ.

How to Create Boundaries

The following are ways on how one can create boundaries:

- *Show love.* Love is a barrier. The love of God for you and His purpose for humanity allowed Him to sacrifice His only begotten Son. Even when the ultimate price of scourging and crucifixion was being meted out to Jesus, the purpose of the Almighty for mankind and His love ensured He ignored the pleas of Jesus. Jesus had to cry out, "My Lord, My God why has thou forsaken me?" Love of your purpose in life will make you forsake anything and even anyone who wants to stand in the way of fulfilling your purpose.
- *Love the Father.* Love must flow from the top for any individual who has the license to succeed. It must start with the love of God (the Father). Even when nobody is physically present, the understanding that there is One who is always present and He determines the course of any man's life will enable you to say, "Why will I do this and sin against my God?" (Gen. 39:9).
- *Love your future.* When you love your future, it will be extremely easy to ignore the juicy baits that will eventually become the bane of a glorious future. Gehazi, the servant of Elisha, did not love his future (2 Kings 5:20–27). Esau did not love his future. He easily and thoughtlessly sold his birthright.
- *Love your family.* Love demands action and sacrifice. The love of your family will prevent any individual from participating in anything that will tarnish the image of the family and bring the family to the abyss of shame and disrepute.
- *Love your friends.* While it is important that you love your friends, you must also be forthright. Some people use the word *faithful* as a form of bondage. You must be able to lovingly let a friend know you will not

watch his or her back when he or she is engaging in unscrupulous acts. Saying no has numerous advantages. It may be the difference between utilizing the license to succeed for the whole world to see and being shackled in the prison. "Wounds made by a friend are intended to help, but an enemy's kisses are too much to bear" (Prov. 27:6, GWT). Never be a lapdog. The love of your friends ensures you do not cheat or defraud them. Do not stab your friend in the back.

Belong

> Then God said, "Let the water under the sky come together in one area, and let the dry land appear." And so it was. God named the dry land earth. The water which came together he named sea. God saw that it was good. Then God said, "Let the earth produce vegetation: plants bearing seeds, each according to its own type, and fruit trees bearing fruit with seeds, each according to its own type." (Gen. 1:9-11, NLT)

God has not created us to be in a vacuum. We have been created to belong. To belong means to be a part of something, to be a member of a group, or to be in a suitable place. It has been mentioned that one of the reasons for the creation of man was so that God would have fellowship with man. This relationship was broken when Adam stepped out of bounds. Enoch filled this vacuum:

> And Enoch walked [in habitual fellowship] with God; and he was not, for God took him [home with Him]. (Gen. 5:24, TAB)

When Jesus was about to start his ministry, he also sought fellowship: "And he ordained twelve, that they should be with him" (Mark 3:14, KJV). Jesus realized that in order for him to become all that his Father purposed him to be, he had to belong to become.

In 1753, a scientist in Sweden named Carolus Linnaeus thought of an orderly system for classifying plants and animals. He grouped all organisms according to a two-part name (binomial). The first part of the name is the "generic" grouping, or genus. The second part is the "specific" grouping, or species. Scientists today still use this basic idea of his system. In order to begin to classify plants, he considered the structure by which the plant absorbs water. Plants are either vascular or nonvascular. Vascular plants have tube-like structures that transport water from the roots to the stem to the leaves. Nonvascular plants absorb water only through their surfaces. Another way he considered plant classification was according to reproduction. Some plants reproduce by producing seeds. Others produce spores.

To begin to classify animals, Carolus Linnaeus considered the backbone. Animals that have a backbone are called vertebrates. Animals that do not have a backbone are called invertebrates. One way to consider groups of vertebrates is according to their diet. Animals that primarily eat plants are known as herbivores. Animals that feed mostly on meat are known as carnivores. Some animals, called omnivores, eat both plants and meat. Another way to consider groups of vertebrates is according to their body temperature. All vertebrates are either cold-blooded or warm-blooded (Franklin Institute).

What Carolus Linnaeus discovered about 250 years ago was put in place by God at Creation: "Let the earth produce after its own kind." In life, everybody is trying to become something or somebody, but the order of heaven is that "you need to belong, before you can become."

You need to become after a kind. If you do not belong, you will not have a kind. In reality, everybody belongs. It now depends on who or what you belong to.

> Live in me. Make your home in me just as I do in you. In the same way that a branch can't bear grapes by itself but only by being joined to the vine, you can't bear fruit unless you are joined with me. I am the Vine, you are the branches. When you're joined with me and I with you, the relation intimate and organic, the harvest is sure to be abundant. Separated, you can't produce a thing. Anyone who separates from me is deadwood, gathered up and thrown on the bonfire. But if you make yourselves at home with me and my words are at home in you, you can be sure that whatever you ask will be listened to and acted upon. (John 15:4–7, MSG)

It is extremely important to God that you truly belong to him for any true transformation to happen in your life or situation. "So you also are complete through your union with Christ, who is the head over every ruler and authority" (Col. 2:10, NLT).

When you look at the Bible, you will see God describing himself and advising we should be like him:

- He wants us to be like Him in spirit. For example, the Word of God says, "God is a spirit and they that worship Him must worship Him in spirit and in truth" (John 4:24, KJV).

  > But you are not controlled by your sinful nature. You are controlled by the Spirit if you have the Spirit of God living in you. (And remember that those who do not have the Spirit of Christ living in them do not belong to him at all.) (Rom. 8:9, NLT)

  > Moreover, we have had earthly fathers who disciplined us and we yielded [to them] and respected [them for training us]. Shall we not much more cheerfully submit to the Father of spirits and so [truly] live? (Heb. 12:9, TAB)

- He wants us to be like Him in love (1 John 4:7–20).
- He wants us to be like Him in giving (John 3:16; 2 Cor. 9:6–7).
- He wants us to be like Him in holiness (Lev. 19:2, Ps. 99:9, Isa. 48:17, Isa. 54:5, 1 Pet. 1:15–16).

When you look at the world system, you find out that a concept that the developed organizations, economies, and countries have perfected is the principle of belonging. This creates a sense of worth, identity, and class. Most of the underdeveloped countries only have a passport as the only meaningful connection between their citizens and the country.

When you contrast that to developed countries with national or social insurance numbers, health cards, driver's licenses, records of birth, etc., you can easily identify yourself as belonging to such a country. This has helped them to promote growth and order because they can easily plan and forecast. This ensures the citizens have pride in their country. It also shows the country cares for her citizens.

Any institution or company that is able to make her workers feel and know they belong will have a high retention rate and output. This was a key to the success of David while running away from Saul. The people in debt, discontent and depressed, gathered themselves unto David, but later on, they were ready to give their life for him. Where society abandoned and discarded them, they were welcomed by David. A sense of belonging creates a close bond of friendship and affection.

Why You Need to Belong

Teamwork makes the dream work. A team comprises of a group of people linked in a common purpose. Teams are especially appropriate for conducting tasks that are high in complexity and have many interdependent subtasks. A group in itself does not necessarily constitute a team. Teams normally have members with complimentary skills and generate synergy through a coordinated effort, which allows each member to maximize his or her strengths and minimize his or her weaknesses.

> Here is one alone—no one with him; he neither has child nor brother. Yet there is no end to all his labor, neither is his eye satisfied with riches, neither does he ask, for whom do I labor and deprive myself of good? This is also vanity (emptiness, falsity, and futility); yes, it is a painful effort and an unhappy business. Two are better than one, because they have a good [more satisfying] reward for their labor; For if they fall, the one will lift up his fellow. But woe to him who is alone when he falls and has not another to lift him up! Again, if two lie down together, then they have warmth; but how can one be warm alone? And though a man might prevail against him who is alone, two will withstand him. A threefold cord is not quickly broken. (Eccles. 4:10–12, TAB)

The following are reasons to belong:

1. *Support.* When you belong, a support system is available for you no matter how relative or minimal. Simeon and Levi supported Dinah when she was raped because she was their sister.

2. *Sustenance.* The care given to Jacob in Egypt and Goshen was because Joseph had been sent ahead to preserve the family. Joseph was the son of Jacob.

3. *Strength.* There are different parts to a tree with varying functions (root, trunk, branches, leaves, etc.). As powerful as the eyes are, the whole body is more important and consequently stronger than the eye.

4. *Security.* There is a measure of protection when you are part of a team than when alone. Boldness is immediately conferred.

5. *Selection.* If David did not belong to the family of Jesse, he would not have been selected. Samuel was sent to the family of Jesse.

6. *Success.* The achievement of one can be contagious. Having a relationship with one person or belonging to a team can immediately lead to a chain reaction of further lofty attainments.

> This is what the Lord of Armies says: In those days ten people from every language found among the nations will take hold of the clothes of a Jew. They will say, "Let us go with you because we have heard that God is with you." (Zech. 8:23, GWT emphasis added)

Here are ways on how to belong:

1. *Say so.* Make your intention known. Moses said to Reuben and Levi, "Who is on the Lord's side?" (Exod. 32:26).

2. *Sign up.* Make a commitment. Elisha signed up in the prophetic school of Elijah (1 Kings 19:19–21).

3. *Sit down.* Make your obedience known. No matter how good you are, learn what obtains in the environment that you have found yourself (Rom. 16:19–20).

4. *Step up.* Be a contributor, not a parasite.

5. *Stand up.* Be willing to defend your team.

6. *Stretch high.* Be willing to learn and sacrifice your time, talent, treasures, etc.

Beauty

> And God saw that this was good (fitting, admirable) and He approved it. (Gen. 10:12b, TAB)

> The soul that sees beauty may sometimes walk alone. (Johann Wolfgang von Goethe)

> Delight yourself also in the Lord, and He will give you the desires and secret petitions of your heart. (Ps. 37:4, TAB)

Beauty can be described as a beautiful person or thing. It can also be more broadly described as the quality present in a thing or person that gives intense pleasure or deep satisfaction to the mind, whether arising from sensory manifestations (as shape, color, sound, etc.).

Most times, the miraculous is wrapped up in the midst of the mundane or ridiculous. After the commandment given to the waters in the book of beginning manifested and God named the outcome, God showed appreciation by saying, "This is fitting and admirable." The pronouncement of God ("This is good") is a confirmation of the goodness he saw before the appearance of the goodness he now sees.

Let me try to break this down. In the midst of the rubble that was earth then, God brought refinement, but before he physically saw the refined product, he already saw it in the spirit. He knew what he wanted to see, and he eventually saw it. It is often said that beauty is in the eye of the beholder. This is because "the soul that sees beauty may sometimes walk alone."

For every level of glory that others are applauding, there is always a story that many have rejected or abandoned. The owner of the story always demonstrates a determination often bordering on stubbornness because he saw the glory or beauty before it appeared. This is because he saw what others could not see.

What you want is hidden in what you have. You have a duty to unveil the treasures in you for the world to see. Seeing beauty in the midst of ashes is a power of not only positive confession but also action. It is important you endeavor to see beauty in what you want to embark upon before you start the journey so that when you arrive at your destination, you will be able to compare if it looks like what you saw.

Something I found unbelievable when I visited the nation of Israel was the arid nature of the land and how mountainous the terrain was. I compared this to the "powerful pronouncement" of Jehovah when He met Moses on the back side of the desert and said,

> And I have come down to deliver them out of the hand and power of the Egyptians and to bring them up out of that land to a land good and large, a land flowing with milk and honey [a land of plenty]—to the place of the Canaanite, the Hittite, the Amorite, the Perizzite, the Hivite, and the Jebusite. (Exod. 3:8, TAB)

This pronouncement of El Shaddai was a statement of faith. The Almighty said the land was good, large but also flowing with milk and honey. The question that comes to mind is, What is the total acreage of the land? Is it one of the largest lands in the world? Has anybody ever seen a land flowing with milk and honey?

Ordinarily, according to the way that God has ordained creation, milk is from cow and honey is from bee. In this instance, is God saying he has reversed the order of things and honey and milk will be spewing from the ground? Looking deeper, the land is supposed to be large, but it was already filled with other nationals—the Canaanites, Hittites, Amorites, Perizzites, Hivites, and Jebusites.

We even say three is a crowd, but by the time you add the Israelites with twelve tribes, you can either say we now have six or seventeen nations living together.

Jehovah Jireh the Great Provider saw things in a different light. In the midst of everything, he saw enlargement that will lead to beauty. He knew that if the mysteries in his pronouncement were mastered, the Israelites will rejoice. This is why He is able to call those things that be not as though they were. What do you see? In the face of turmoil, do you see triumph? In the midst of confusion, do you see conquest, and in the midst of ashes, do you see beauty?

Concerning your situation, circumstance, and challenges at the moment, God sees things in a different light. He knows that from whatever you are going through, you shall yet praise Him.

> To grant [consolation and joy] to those who mourn in Zion—to give them an ornament (a garland or diadem) of beauty instead of ashes, the oil of joy instead of mourning, the garment [expressive] of praise instead of a heavy, burdened, and failing spirit—that they may be called oaks of righteousness [lofty, strong, and magnificent, distinguished for uprightness, justice, and right standing with God], the planting of the Lord, that He may be glorified. And they shall rebuild the ancient ruins; they shall raise up the former desolations and renew the ruined cities, the devastations of many generations. Aliens shall stand [ready] and feed your flocks, and foreigners shall be your plowmen and your vinedressers. But you shall be called the priests of the Lord; people will speak of you as the ministers of our God. You shall eat the wealth of the nations, and the glory [once that of your captors] shall be yours. Instead of your [former] shame you shall have a twofold recompense; instead of dishonor and reproach [your people] shall rejoice in their portion. Therefore, in their land they shall possess double [what they had forfeited]; everlasting joy shall be theirs. (Isa. 61:3–7, TAB)

There is the story of a woman—popularly called the Shunamite woman—that demonstrated a perceiving mentality: able to discern that the man passing by was a servant of God. A promoting attitude—hospitality, positive confession—instead of death saw life and also had a powerful resolve not to quit, and her desire was eventually granted. She had her gaze fixed on the miracle working power of the Most High God (2 Kings 4:8–37).

That situation that you are in "is good" because after the processing of the vegetable called bitter leaf comes a sweet delicacy. All things will eventually work together for your good.

It may seem as if you have come to the end of the road now, but God will make a way where there seems to be no way, because He works in ways you cannot see. Even if you cannot see it in the physical, please see it with the eyes of the mind.

God met a man and told him to leave everything he had been used to. He left not knowing the place he was going to. God said He would show him where he will go as he goes. What a command. This man obeyed God. The Bible mentioned this:

> By an act of faith, Abraham said yes to God's call to travel to an unknown place that would become his home. When he left he had no idea where he was going. By an act of faith he lived in the country promised him, lived as a stranger camping in tents. Isaac and Jacob did the same, living under the same promise. Abraham did it by keeping his eye on an unseen city with real, eternal foundations—the City designed and built by God. (Heb. 11:8–10, MSG)

As the story unfolds, God even made some promises to him, but Abraham had no child until he was almost a hundred years old. Then came a supreme test—for Abraham to go and sacrifice this child—and he readily obeyed. Why did he obey without question, and also completely? Because he knew that God is a beautiful God, and in the midst of it all, beauty will show up.

This was why Abraham told the servants,

> Stay here with the donkey. The boy and I will travel a little farther. We will worship there, and then "*we*" will come right back." (Gen. 22:5, NLT)

Notice that Abraham had the staunch belief that he and Isaac will come back. Ralph Waldo Emerson said, "Though we travel the world over to find the beautiful, we must carry it with us or we will find it not."

I believe it will be right for us to ponder where God got the vocabulary *good* from. A quick retort from a whole lot of people is, "But He is God." A deeper look would be, "He had it in Him already." He is an embodiment of everything good. He was carrying good all around. That is why we can say God is good.

Moses said, God has promised us good, let us do you good. Good is God unto Israel. Every good and perfect gift comes from him.

Remember the song "God is Good" by Don Moen. He is good all the time.

That situation that looks grave can be good if you carry the beautiful in you.

> No matter how much you seek the beautiful, if you do not carry beauty in you, when you even find it, you will not know it because you do not know what it looks like.

God, the creator of heaven and earth could say it was good because He knew what good looks like. He had been looking forward to good. He had the picture of good in His mind so that when He saw it, he recognized it. What picture are you carrying about in your mind? Is it doom and gloom?

Here is how to see beauty in the midst of ashes:

- Realize that you cannot change the past.

> "Hast thou faith? have it to thyself before God. Happy is he that condemneth not himself in that thing which he alloweth" (Rom. 14:22, KJV).

- Realize that the promise of God is not dependent on the ashes.

> But things have changed. I'm taking the side of my core of surviving people: Sowing and harvesting will resume, Vines will grow grapes, Gardens will flourish, Dew and rain will make everything green. "My core survivors will get everything they need—and more. You've gotten a reputation as a bad-news people, you people of Judah and Israel, but I'm coming to save you. From now on, you're the good-news people. Don't be afraid. Keep a firm grip on what I'm doing." A Message from God-of-the-Angel-Armies: "In the same way that I decided to punish you when your ancestors made me angry, and didn't pull my punches, at this time I've decided to bless Jerusalem and the country of Judah. Don't be afraid." (Zech. 8:11–15, MSG)

- Realize your role, and do not doubt him.

  > If they had been thinking about the country that they had left, they could have found a way to go back. Instead, these men were longing for a better country—a heavenly country. That is why God is not ashamed to be called their God. He has prepared a city for them. (Heb. 11:15–16, GWT)

- Realize that it is neither by your power nor might.

  > Then he said to me, "This is what the LORD says to Zerubbabel: It is not by force nor by strength, but by my Spirit, says the LORD of Heaven's Armies. Nothing, not even a mighty mountain, will stand in Zerubbabel's way; it will become a level plain before him! And when Zerubbabel sets the final stone of the Temple in place, the people will shout: 'May God bless it! May God bless it!'" (Zech. 4:6–7, NLT)

- Realize that it is not too bad or too late for God.

  > The LORD kept his word and did for Sarah exactly what he had promised. She became pregnant, and she gave birth to a son for Abraham in his old age. This happened at just the time God had said it would. (Gen. 21:1–2, NLT)

Beware

> And God made the [wild] beasts of the earth according to their kinds, and domestic animals according to their kinds, and everything that creeps upon the earth according to its kind. And God saw that it was good (fitting, pleasant) and He approved it. (Gen. 1:25, TAB)

The word *beware* means to be cautious, on guard, or wary. It is a word of wisdom (Prov. 3:19–24). It is interesting to note that as God was transforming the land that was void and without shape, He was creating seas, oceans, and wild animals. At the end, He looked at them and said it was good.

Ordinarily, we know that a whole lot of people will run away if an elephant or lion enters the auditorium that you are in; even some will run if they see a rat. The same God that created man also created these animals. This God created not only domestic animals but also wild ones.

A look at the Word of God reveals many things:

> See, it is I who created the blacksmith who fans the coals into flame and forges a weapon fit for its work. And it is I who have created the destroyer to work havoc. (Isa. 54:16, TNIV)

Many people do not know this verse in the Bible, but it is between two popular ones that majority of kingdom citizens know.

Isaiah 54:15 (KJV) says, "Behold, they shall surely gather together, but not by me: whosoever shall gather together against thee shall fall for thy sake." Verse 17 says, "No weapon that is formed against thee shall prosper; and every tongue that shall rise against thee in judgment thou shalt condemn. This is the heritage of the servants of the LORD, and their righteousness is of me, saith the LORD."

We know what is in verses 15 and 17, but we don't know what is in verse 16. This is the main reason why we have to beware. It is the same Word of God that says there could be a gathering but if the gathering is not organized by him, all those that gather against you shall fall. That also says no weapons that is formed or fashioned against you shall prosper. The question is, what if He is the one that created the weapon or organized the gathering?

At least He boldly said, "He has created the waster to destroy." What I am trying to get across is that in as much as you seek to evolve, ensure it is in line with the will of God. It is the same God who created domestic animals who also created wild animals. Why did he create wild animals? These are animals that eat other animals, and some of them do eat men.

> So he gave them what they asked for, but he sent a plague along with it. (Ps. 106:15, NLT)

In the book of Numbers, the Israelites murmured against Moses and God that they were eating all manner of delicacy in Egypt but since leaving Egypt all they had to eat was "this manna." In short, the Israelites sought to evolve, and God granted them their request, but alongside came plague (Num. 11:4–33).

It is the blessing of the Lord that makes rich and He adds no sorrow to it.

Beware of what you ask from the Lord. At a time, the Israelites requested for a king like other nations. The prophet of that time, Samuel, was very upset, and he was dejected until God consoled him that the Israelites did not reject him but God.

The Israelites were then told the outcome of having a king (1 Sam. 8:4–20), but they still wanted a king so that they will be like other nations.

Why do you seek the transformation that you are calling unto God for? Is it to be like others? Is it for you to reject the King of kings? In the quest for a transformation, be cautious.

Not everybody who laughs with you is happy with you.

The same people who cry hosanna today will cry crucify him tomorrow if the price is right. If you are not sure, ask our Lord Jesus.

Why Do You Need to Beware?

Here are the reasons why we need to be wary:

1. Understand there is always more to whatever you see or seek in life.

> When Pharaoh let the people go, God led them not by way of the land of the Philistines, although that was nearer; for God said, Lest the people change their purpose when they see war and return to Egypt. (Exod. 13:17, TAB)

> But I will not drive them out in a single year, because the land would become desolate and the wild animals would multiply and threaten you. I will drive them out a little at a time until your population has increased enough to take possession of the land. (Exod. 23:29–30, NLT)

2. Understand that He knows the motive behind the evolving that you seek.

> Elisha stared at Hazael with a fixed gaze until Hazael became uneasy. Then the man of God started weeping. "What's the matter, my lord?" Hazael asked him. Elisha replied, "I know the terrible things you will do to the people of Israel. You will burn their fortified cities, kill their young men with the sword, dash their little children to the ground, and rip open their pregnant women!" (2 Kings 8:11–12, NLT)

3. Understand that He alone knows what you are supposed to be (e.g., Elisha following Elijah, Abraham leaving all, Peter leaving all the fish, Saul asking the question "What do you want me to do?").

4. Understand that He alone knows the true path to evolving.

> O Lord [pleads Jeremiah in the name of the people], I know that [the determination of] the way of a man is not in himself; it is not in man [even in a strong man or in a man at his best] to direct his [own] steps. (Jer. 10:23, TAB [e.g., Jonah sent to Nineveh but started going to Tarshish])

5. Understand that others are also seeking to evolve.

> While they were at the great rock in Gibeon, Amasa came to meet them. Joab was wearing his military tunic, and strapped over it at his waist was a belt with a dagger in its sheath. As he stepped forward, it dropped out of its sheath. Joab said to Amasa, "How are you, my brother?" Then Joab took Amasa by the beard with his right hand to kiss him. Amasa was not on his guard against the dagger in Joab's hand, and Joab plunged it into his belly, and his intestines spilled out on the ground. Without being stabbed again, Amasa died. Then Joab and his brother Abishai pursued Sheba son of Bikri. (2 Sam. 20:8–10, TNIV)

What Should You Beware?

Here are the things you should be beware:

1. *Procrastination.* It delays (Prov. 24:30–34).

2. *People.* They derail (e.g., people in the life of King Saul) (1 Sam. 15: 21, 1 Sam. 18:6–7).

3. *Power.* It intoxicates. It leads to greed, as with King Ahab and Jezebel (1 Kings 21:1–14) and King David, Bathsheba, and Uriah (2 Sam. 11:1–27).

4. *Pride.* It sets you against God—for example, Lucifer (Isa. 14:12–15, 1 Pet. 5:5, James 4:6).

Here are ways on how to beware:

1. *Pray.* Keeps you in check. "And in the morning, long before daylight, He got up and went out to a deserted place, and there He prayed" (Mark 1:35, TAB).

2. *Praise.* Keeps you in contact. "My heart is fixed, O God, my heart is fixed: I will sing and give praise" (Ps. 57:7, KJV).

3. *Purpose.* Keeps you in tune.

> This was John's testimony when the Jewish leaders sent priests and Temple assistants from Jerusalem to ask John, "Who are you?" He came right out and said, "I am not the Messiah." "Well then, who are you?" they asked. "Are you Elijah?" "No," he replied. "Are you the Prophet we are expecting?" "No." "Then who are you? We need an answer for those who sent us. What do you have to say about yourself?" John replied in the words of the prophet Isaiah: "I am a voice shouting in the wilderness, 'Clear the way for the Lord's coming!'" (John 1:19–23, NLT; John 3:25–28)

4. *Pursuit.* Keeps you on track. "We must work the works of Him Who sent Me and be busy with His business while it is daylight; night is coming on, when no man can work" (John 9:4, TAB).

Behold

The word *behold* can mean to perceive by the visual or mental faculty, to look upon or gaze at (i.e., to see). The first occurrence of the word *behold* in the Bible was when God mentioned all the things that He had done (i.e., the evolving that had taken place [Gen. 1:29]), and the next occurrence was of God looking over everything and giving a stamp of approval.

> And God saw everything that He had made, and behold, it was very good (suitable, pleasant) and He approved it completely. And there was evening and there was morning, a sixth day. (Gen. 1:31, TAB)

The ability to behold is very important in a journey of evolving. It moves you from the group of people that do things by trial and error. It can be the difference between a denied, delayed, and distinct change or evolving.

Hunters sometimes use dogs to assist them in hunting their prey. There is a type that is called a hound. The hounds are further divided into either scent or sight hounds. The scent hounds smell out their prey while the sight hounds see the prey afar off. This is a special ability that assists them in cornering or hounding their prey long before the prey even knows they are being stalked.

When you look at this analogy relative to a key ingredient (ability to behold) that must be present for evolving you can liken it to a skill, knack, or capacity to "know" what needs to be done or the right path to take, recognize the agent through which evolving takes place, or even know the place to evolve. In a nutshell, it can be described as being able to see, scent, or sound what, where, or how your blessings look like in the spiritual and confirm it in the physical.

Such abilities come by way of persistent training. It is an ability that becomes inherent in you due to the fact that you have consistently educated your faculties to know "what the trail of victory looks like." When you get to such a point, you do not have to actually have a confirmation from anybody.

Let us look at these three examples. The first one is Abraham. At a time, Abraham was given a tough assignment—to sacrifice his only son. By the grace of God, he complied. The instruction in itself was not explicit:

> He said, "Take your dear son Isaac whom you love and go to the land of Moriah. Sacrifice him there as a burnt offering on one of the mountains that I'll point out to you." (Gen. 22:2, MSG)

Subsequently in this chapter, it should have been recorded that God actually pointed out the exact mountain to Abraham, but the next thing that we read is, "On the third day of their journey, Abraham looked up and saw the place in the distance" (Gen. 22:4, NLT). Wait a minute, how can this be possible? If we assume there was a banner or signpost that said "Welcome to Moriah," was there a signpost that also said "Welcome to Mount Moriah"? How did Abraham locate this place?

In fact, the instruction was, "I will point out the place." Though it was not recorded that the place was pointed out to Abraham, but when he saw the place, he knew the place. Abraham beheld the place. There was divine confirmation within him that that was the place. When you behold, you may not be able to explain it, you just know. People may ask you, "How do you know?" and you will just tell them, "I just know." The ability "to just know" is a needed prerequisite for true evolving. This ability is developed over time based on consistent communion with the King of kings. Sometimes, it may just not be one thing but a series of events or occurrence that you have seen through the eyes of God in time past that brings about such a confirmation. The ability to behold changes your language and attitude.

After Abraham saw the place from a distance, he told his servants, "Stay here with the donkey." Abraham told the servants. "The boy and I will travel a little farther. We will worship there, and then we will come right back" (Gen. 22:5, NLT). Abraham spoke convincingly based on his ability to behold the goodness and mercies of God. Whatever is named by good and pleasant that has left you is coming right back in Jesus's name, amen. Whatever the King of glory has divinely joined to you and your destiny, intricately woven together to bring praise and glory to His holy name that has slipped away or eluded you, is coming right back.

Let me tell you something critical: when Noah was told to build an ark and he complied, all those who were supposed to be in the boat got in and God divinely closed the door. Every door of shame and sorrow has been closed concerning you in Jesus's name, amen.

God specifically told Noah to take two animals (male and female) from all the animal types (species) in the world then. God gave this instruction knowing fully well there will be mating, union, consummation. This will bring about progeny or offspring. This immediately tells me that more animals came out of the boat than those that went in. In the midst of the confusion, or your so-called troubles, God is working it out. The Holy Spirit is brooding over you to birth a glorious future. You cannot go out the same way that you went in.

That trouble or challenge will leave you better than you were before. Problems birth progress, you will progress. You will move forward. You will wax great. You will become exceedingly great in Jesus's name. The rain came (the rain is coming be prepared), but after the rain fulfilled its assignment, it stopped, and the flood receded.

Among the animals that were in the boat with Noah was a bird called a raven that God already prepared for a special assignment. The Bible records that the raven went back and forth (Gen. 8:7). Because something or someone has gone does not mean it or they will not come back. Whatever destiny has joined to you that will oil your wheel of progress, though gone, is coming back in the mighty name of Jesus. God has made provision for your vision.

At every level of progress are levels of resources. Even when it seemed as if the raven had completed its assignment, the dove immediately took over. You will never lack the goodness of heaven. It is interesting to find out a dove took over from a raven. A raven is a bird of mysterious character while a dove is the opposite. God is changing every raven to a dove in your life in Jesus's name, amen. That which is crooked is becoming straight, and that which is rough is becoming smooth.

Our second example is the woman of Shunem. The Bible records,

> And she said to her husband, Behold now, I perceive that this is a holy man of God who passes by continually. (2 Kings 4:9, TAB)

Nobody told this woman, she just sensed it. You need to develop the ability to sense your evolving when you see it.

We do not know how she sensed it. Maybe she scented, sounded, or saw. All we do know based on the Bible is that she sensed it. It does not matter how she sensed it. In the preceding verse, the Word of God mentions that this woman urged, constrained, or insisted that Elisha should eat in her house. Why did she do this?

It was not only Elisha that walked on the street. Even then, when she asked Elisha to stop by to eat, Elisha refused. She had to insist or constrain him. The Word of God says that this woman was wealthy and influential. She could have been offended or snobbish, but she still insisted Elisha eat in her house. Why go through all these? She saw what others could not see.

A careful reflection on this story tells me that she already knew Elisha was a man of God. The account in verse 9 was just to tell her husband what she found out. She already knew. When you behold and you begin to insist, urge, or constrain the one or thing you beheld, it ensures you do not miss your opportunity or season of rejoicing.

There are some articles that are known as "diamond in the rough." To everybody, it is worthless, but for those who can behold, it is a diamond that needs cutting and polishing. May you see your diamond, even in the midst of debris, when you come across it in Jesus's name, amen.

> There is a miracle in your misery, treasures in your troubles, possibilities in your problems, triumph in your travail, prosperity in your poverty, honour in your humiliation and power in your pressures. (Rev. P. J. A. Olaiya)

As this story unfolds, you will notice that because of what she knew, her attitude and her language changed when she faced adversity. The man of God whom this Shunammite woman took care of later became a channel of blessing because according to the prophecy given by Elisha, she had a child at the exact time prophesied. Later on, this child died, but the woman held unto a firm belief that this child would resurrect. She kept on repeating that "it is well," and it was eventually well with her and her household because the dead came to life.

This is what can happen when you truly behold the goodness of the Lord. You are convinced there is yet hope for a tree if it be cut down that it will spring again. You are able to do like Abraham, "you hope against hope." What you behold will ensure you are able to deal with the storms of life appropriately and effectively.

Our third example is Elijah the Tishbite of the inhabitants of Gilead. On a particular day, he just made a simple proclamation that there will not be rain for years, and heaven sanctioned the command. After cleansing the land of Israel of idolatry by slaying the agents of darkness and doom in the persons of the prophets of Baal, he made another statement: "There is a sound of abundance of rain." Wow, he did not say that there is sound of rain but that of abundance. He heard the sound. Can you hear the sound of your abundance?

At that time, there had been no rain for a long time; there was no cloud rumbling of thunder either, and the land had been arid for a while, but in the midst of all these difficulties—when everybody could only see, scent, or sound famine—he heard the sound of abundance. Abundance is on the way for you in Jesus's name, amen. The sound he heard affected his attitude and the subsequent instruction that he issued later on to King Ahab, "Go and rejoice."

The word *behold* is a link to your destiny.

> When Jesus therefore saw his mother, and the disciple standing by, whom he loved, he saith unto his mother, Woman, behold thy son! Then saith he to the disciple, Behold thy mother! And from that hour that disciple took her unto his own home. (John 19:26–27, KJV)

A relationship that both Mary and John could not fathom was initiated because somebody saw it happening and he transferred what he saw to them. When Jesus introduced what was about to begin to both of them, they did not complain. Mary could have said, "What about Joseph, my husband? How about your other brothers? Won't I become a burden to this John of a fellow? Where am I going to stay in his house? Will his mother not be jealous of this relationship? How do I deal with his wife?" These are all valid questions any mind could conceive.

Even John could also be thinking, "I already have a mother. What do I want to do with two mothers? How am I going to feed them?" But from that very moment, John took her into his own home. A lifelong relationship started. A destiny-changing relationship was started.

Is it possible that it was because of a relationship like this that among all the disciples it was only John who died a natural death, and also got the profound revelations that resulted into the book of Revelation in the Bible? In your journey toward transformation, ensure you are always developing relationships that will be a link toward your destiny. You have to deliberately cultivate relationships with a purpose in mind.

Behold is a statement of victory on this earth and in eternity (i.e., what you have been expecting for a long time has finally happened). This means you need to behold your victory. A song says the following: "Behold he comes, Riding on the clouds…". By the mercy of God, salvation is coming your way in that situation no matter how unpleasant.

Behold is a word of joy, exaltation, and thanksgiving. You will thank the Lord in this season in Jesus's name.

How Do You Behold?

Here are ways to behold:

- Spend time doing good. Shepherds watched their flocks by night (Matt. 2:1–2), Job took care of the motherless (Job 29:1–12), Cornelius gave alms (Acts 10:4), Dorcas wove.
- Spend time in His presence, like Elijah did on the mountain (2 Kings 1:9), how Paul and Silas prayed (Acts 16:25–26). A staff blossomed in His presence (Num. 17:4–8).
- Spend time in His service. Zechariah served in the temple (Luke 1:5–12).
- Spend time seeking holiness (Heb. 12:14).

The Components

> For these things took place, that the Scripture might be fulfilled (verified, carried out), Not one of His bones shall be broken. (John 19:36, TAB)

To operate effectively with your license, you have to clearly understand the relevant components and excellently pursue them—take "His bones" with you wherever you go and in whatever you do.

In anatomy or zoology, a bone literally is one of the structures composing the skeleton of a vertebrate. It is the hard-connective tissue forming the substance of the skeleton of most vertebrates and impregnated with calcium, phosphate, and other minerals. Idiomatically, the word *bone* is used to express different situations, as in the following:

- *Bone up.* To study intensely.
- *Keep a stern outlook.* To harden one's expression
- *Feel in one's bone.* To think or feel intuitively.
- *Have a bone to pick.* To have cause to disagree or argue with someone.
- *Make no bones about.* To deal with in a direct manner.
- *To the bone.* To the essentials, minimum or extreme degree.

Most often in the Bible, the occurrence of the word *bone* metaphorically or figuratively **symbolizes Strength:**

Then Elisha died and was buried. Groups of Moabite raiders used to invade the land each spring. Once when some Israelites were burying a man, they spied a band of these raiders. So they hastily threw the corpse into the tomb of Elisha and fled. But as soon as the body touched Elisha's bones, the dead man revived and jumped to his feet! (2 Kings 13:20–21, NLT)

In our zoological definition of *bone*, the word *impregnated* came up. While our bones in the physical are impregnated with minerals, in the spiritual, it is the extent of our holiness and divine connection that determines the content and subsequently the strength of our bones. At a time in the Bible, a man of God passed away, and by the law of decay, the flesh and other spongy tissues will be the first to decompose: "And after my body (flesh) has decayed" (Job 19:26, NLT).

After the decomposition of the flesh of this man of God, there remained the bones. The Bible mentions to us that there was a time that a dirge was being sung and the burial procession came to the tomb of this man of God. At this juncture and by worldly comprehension, the events that unfolded could be deemed a coincidence. This is because there was an uproar because of some incorrigible miscreants from Moab that came to raid Israel, and due to fear, the burial procession dropped the corpse in the tomb and waited a minute upon the bones of the man of God, Elisha. Coincidence, isn't it?

While the world will call this a coincidence, it was actually a divine arrangement because the man—Elisha—still had an outstanding assignment he did not carry out while alive to fulfill his destiny. Elisha received the double portion of the anointing of Elijah, and he had to perform double the miracles of Elijah. Also, the unnamed man who was about to be buried had things to do alive. Therefore, he had to be resurrected. You will not die before your time in Jesus's name.

Every word of prophesy concerning your life shall not go unfulfilled. This man stood up on his feet after his corpse came in contact with the bones of Elisha. What was in the bone of Elisha? Definitely at this time it cannot be calcium, phosphates, or other nutrients.

There had to be divine deposits capable of resurrecting a dead man to the point that this man was able to stand on his feet after he had been dead for a number of days. Divine electricity or anointing latent in the bones of Elisha became kinetic after the dead corpse touched the bone. Despite the fact Elisha was dead in the physical, his bones were still alive. So this was a case of the living—bone coming in contact with the dead. It was a situation of light—bone coming in contact with darkness. Light overpowered darkness. The divine strength in the bone caused the sting of death to be impotent.

Satan, in his attempt to destroy Job, told Jehovah Hoseenu, "But put forth Your hand now, and touch his bone and his flesh, and he will curse and renounce You to Your face" (Job 2:5, TAB).

You will see here a differentiation of the body into flesh and bones. While the flesh represents the superficial, the bones represent the substance or profound. The statement of Satan was an attempt at a thorough extermination of Job; he could simply have said *body*, but he wanted the place of strength destroyed so that Job will not have any form of defense. It is crucial that you know that in the language of heaven *bone* means "strength."

In effect, wherever you go and wherever you are, ensure that you know His strength is with you.

The word *bone* in the Bible also **symbolizes Safety or Security**:

> The LORD took hold of me, and I was carried away by the Spirit of the LORD to a valley filled with bones. Then he said to me, "Speak a prophetic message to these bones and say, 'Dry bones, listen to the word of the LORD!'" So I spoke the message as he commanded me, and breath came into their bodies. They all came to life and stood up on their feet—a great army. (Ezek. 37:1, 4, 10; TAB)

Ezekiel was one of the Old Testament prophets versed in theology.

> The book of Ezekiel is a morality tale—a sobering reminder of what happens when human creatures declare their independence from their Creator. It's a love story—chronicling God's stubborn affection for his unfaithful people. Best of all, it's a true-life fairy tale, a drama of ultimate redemption—the Hero rescuing his beauty just in the nick of time and making plans to live with her happily ever after. (Integrity Daily Devotional Bible)

Ezekiel had been immersed in religious studies from a young age, so he knew the importance of signs and numbers as it relates to things past, present, and to come. His immersion in religion led to an immunity of sorts from actual world occurrence. As a captive in Babylon, he was able to have a glimpse of what really obtains in the real world outside of the scholarly environment for the first time. What he saw led to his transfixion for seven (perfection) days by the river of Chebar (Ezek. 3:15).

> He was like a bunny brought into the limelight by a car's headlight. He was not used to the wanton disregard of God, His principles and the accompanying orgies. Ezekiel was given some weird tasks by Jehovah El-Gibbor (the Almighty) and for most of them he complied readily. One of such tasks was to lie on his left side for 390 days bearing the sin of Israel and then he was expected to lie on his right side for 40 days for a total of 430 days (Ezek. 4:5–6). Everyday represented a year. For a casual person this seems insane but to Ezekiel this was an insight—an insight into an impending deliverance. The 430 days symbolizes the years of captivity of Israel in Egypt and afterwards there was deliverance from Pharaoh. Ezekiel knew that his action was a prelude to deliverance. (Bishop Tudor Bismark)

So to somebody like Ezekiel, he knew the days of captivity were over. Later on, we also saw Ezekiel being taken to the valley of dry bones, and God asked the question, "Can these dry bones live?" Subsequent prophesy turned the dry bones to a mighty army. An army implies safety, security, or defense.

In verse 11 of Ezekiel 37, the Bible says,

> Son of man, these bones represents the people of Israel. They are saying, we have become old, dry bones—all hope is gone…O my people, I will open your graves of exile and cause you to rise again.

In essence, when the Israelites then were saying all hope was gone, it had its origin in fear. They had become defenseless; their enemies at that time ambushed them at will. Those who were not taken to Babylon were living in servitude.

One of the reasons why you are fearful, worrisome, and sleepless is because you feel defenseless and insecure.

> I will both lay me down in peace, and sleep: for thou, LORD, only makest me dwell in safety. (Ps. 4:8, KJV)

The Israelites were defenseless because of sin, so they were taken into captivity, but God used the illustration of bone to describe security. So therefore, the bone is a symbol of security or safety.

> Thou hast clothed me with skin and flesh, and hast fenced me with bones and sinews. (Job 10:11, KJV)

A fence here is used to describe a bone, and a fence is a symbol of safety or security. In the midst of difficulties, know you have His bones. This should immediately make you secure and safe.

Bone symbolizes Sameness or Similarity:

> And the rib or part of his side which the Lord God had taken from the man He built up and made into a woman, and He brought her to the man. Then Adam said, This [creature] is now bone of my bones and flesh of my flesh; she shall be called Woman, because she was taken out of a man. (Gen. 2:22–23, TAB)

When Adam was placed in the Garden of Eden (Gen. 2:15) and he moved from positional to functional existence, God realized the essence of Adam's creation was not being fulfilled (Gen. 2:18). He therefore brought different kind of animals to Adam so that he could name them. Adam gave names to all the animals, but for himself, he had no companion to name.

Some wonderful principles from this story are the following:

1. God will bring options into your life to see if you will settle for less or go for the best.

2. It is what you call your situation that will manifest. If you call your situation a tiger or beast, the attribute of a beast is readily attached to that situation or person.

3. What you have is enough for God to work with.

4. If what you have is not what you want, make what you want.

Afterward, Jehovah Elohim (the Eternal Creator) caused Adam to fall into a deep sleep, and he took one of Adam's ribs and created a living being from that part. When Adam sighted this creation, he exclaimed in awe and fulfillment, "She is part of my own flesh and bone! She will be called woman" (Gen. 2:23, NLT).

Sameness is the state or quality of being the same—alike, similar, oneness.

When the illustration that bone signifies oneness is used, it means, "What is present in one is present in the other. What one can do, the other can also do. What cannot stop one cannot stop the other."

> For we are members of his body, of his flesh, and of his bones. (Eph. 5:30, KJV)

What Jesus did, you can also do.

> I assure you, most solemnly I tell you, if anyone steadfastly believes in Me, he will himself be able to do the things that I do; and he will do even greater things than these, because I go to the Father. (John 14:12, TAB)

The wonderful attributes of Jesus are also present in you.

> I have strength for all things in Christ Who empowers me [I am ready for anything and equal to anything through Him Who infuses inner strength into me; I am self-sufficient in Christ's sufficiency]. (Phil. 4:13, TAB)

What could not stop Jesus cannot stop you.

> No, the wisdom we speak of is the mystery of God—his plan that was previously hidden, even though he made it for our ultimate glory before the world began. But the rulers of this world have not understood it; if they had, they would not have crucified our glorious Lord. (1 Cor. 2:7–8, NLT)

The Components

Bone also **symbolizes Systems:**

> Then Joseph made the sons of Israel swear an oath, and he said, "When God comes to help you and lead you back, you must take my bones with you." (Gen. 50:25, NLT)

A system is a group of interacting, interrelated, or interdependent elements forming a complex whole. It is an organized set of interrelated ideas or principles that leads to a condition of harmonious orderly interaction. It is also a coordinated method or procedure of achieving an objective. Everything that God created answers to a system. When you get the system right, you get success right away.

There is the solar system in the cosmos and the ecosystem. In anatomy, the body has nervous, reproductive, and skeletal systems. When there is a problem with the nervous system in humans, you have a nervous breakdown. A glitch in the reproductive system leads to reproductive inability while non-coordination of the skeletal system leads to paralysis.

Mechanically every engine or mechanical contraption operates through the avenue of a system (e.g., piston and ring, pulleys and gears, etc.).

Electrically you have the battery and ignition, the grid system, etc.

In government, there is a social, political, health, and economic system. Some are parliamentarian while others are legislative. Other countries still embrace communism while others have democracy.

Even in water filtration, you can have osmosis and reverse osmosis.

In computers, you also have various operating systems (OS) while some are Windows based, others are UNIX or Solaris based.

Everything in life responds to a system. When you function outside of the system, you have chaos, anarchy, disorder, sorrow, lack, distress, and pain.

Once upon a time, a king had a dream, but he did not know what it meant. Due to the fact he did not know what it meant, he did not know what to do with it. He related this dream to his known wise men and astrologers, but none of them could give a meaningful interpretation.

By divine remembrance, a man who was physically incarcerated was brought to interpret this dream. This dream was simply a system of deliverance out of destruction, or what I will call a system of wealth building and sustaining.

So, Pharaoh needs to look for a wise and experienced man and put him in charge of the country. Then Pharaoh needs to appoint managers throughout the country of Egypt to organize it during the years of plenty. Their job will be to collect all the food produced in the good years ahead and stockpile the grain under Pharaoh's authority, storing it in the towns for food. This grain will be held back to be used later during the seven years of famine that are coming on Egypt. This way the country won't be devastated by the famine." This seemed like a good idea to Pharaoh and his officials. Then Pharaoh said to his officials, *"Isn't this the man we need? Are we going to find anyone else who has God's spirit in him like this?"*

So Pharaoh said to Joseph, "*You're the man for us. God has given you the inside story—no one is as qualified as you in experience and wisdom.* From now on, you're in charge of my affairs; all my people will report to you. Only as king will I be over you." So Pharaoh commissioned Joseph: "I'm putting you in charge of the entire country of Egypt." Then Pharaoh removed his signet ring from his finger and slipped it on Joseph's hand. He outfitted him in robes of the best linen and put a gold chain around his neck. He put the second-in-command chariot at his disposal, and as he rode people shouted "Bravo!" Joseph was in charge of the entire country of Egypt. (Gen. 41:33–43, MSG emphasis mine)

Joseph in the land of Egypt was given the inside story (i.e., the system of wealth building). May God give you the inside story for your abundance out of every predicament of life in Jesus's name. When Joseph started implementing this system, Egypt became the lone superpower in the world at that time. Joseph was the man with the experience and wisdom.

One of the questions that came to my mind in reading the above passage is "what experience did Joseph have in ruling a country or coordinating a business enterprise?" The immediate answer is none. We could say, "but he did take care of the house of Potiphar and was also very useful while in the prison." But such experience was not really commensurate to the advertised position: prime minister of Egypt.

The Components

Joseph was the one who actually set the bar: "So, Pharaoh needs to look for a wise and experienced man and put him in charge of the country." While we could say he was qualified in one of the two main criteria that he outlined, but in experience, he was not. It is interesting that the king said no one was qualified as Joseph in wisdom and experience. What is really going on?

Let me try to unravel this. In studying the autobiography of those in great positions of leadership and are functioning excellently, I discovered that they all have a common experience—hardship. When you have gone through challenges, the wisdom with which you deal with any situation is unimaginable. You are able to combine the cerebral with the visceral. You offer advice not only from the brain but also from the heart. For any man or woman with such experience, the spirit will be in perfect union with the ideas that you propose, and there is a divine explosion.

Instead of Joseph being disqualified for lack of experience, it actually showcased him because Pharaoh knew there was none better than Joseph based on what he had gone through in life.

Due to the fact that Joseph had the license to succeed, he became a part of the inner circle of God; therefore, he was privy to the inside story of the system of wealth creation, building, and sustenance despite the fact that he was in prison.

God has a way of sending you to what you have been delivered from—a worthwhile experience.

> Delivering thee from the people, and from the Gentiles, unto whom now I send thee. (Acts 26:17, KJV)

Let me prophesy into your life as you read this book that what you have gone through or are going through is only preparing you for where you are supposed to be. You may have been a drug addict, but there is divine achievement around the corner. You could have been characterized as a harlot or prostitute; maybe you have not read about Rahab. The redemption power of God is available for you. Receive it now in Jesus's name.

As Joseph worked the system, the system worked for him and Egypt. Because of his long stay at the helm of affairs in Egypt, others started understanding the system, and it was working for them. Then Joseph died;

the king of Egypt at that time also died, and a new king came to the throne. Here is the testimony of the new king:

> Now there arose up a new king over Egypt, which knew not Joseph. And he said unto his people, Behold, the people of the children of Israel are more and mightier than we: Come on, let us deal wisely with them; lest they multiply, and it come to pass, that, when there falleth out any war, they join also unto our enemies, and fight against us, and so get them up out of the land. Therefore they did set over them taskmasters to afflict them with their burde,ns. And they built for Pharaoh treasure cities, Pithom and Raamses. (Exod. 1:8–11, KJV)

When Joseph met with the king of Egypt at that time, after he interpreted the dream of the king, a conclusion that this king came to was, "You're the man for us. God has given you the inside story—no one is as qualified as you in experience and wisdom." The king at that time recognized the wisdom of Joseph. This wisdom was so ingrained in him that after his death, the wisdom with its system of wealth building and sustenance was still in Egypt. This was transmitted to the new king because Joseph's bone was upon the soil and this king partook of the wisdom.

This was what led to his statement "Let us deal wisely with them." When an individual does not understand the system of wealth building instead of goodness and mercy to follow, he will be running after goodness and mercy. Such an individual becomes a task worker, managed by taskmasters, afflicted with burdens, and building treasure cities for others while he is unable to build anything for himself and his family.

Since Joseph was the one whom God used to build the system, he also had an insight into what would happen after his demise. This informed his instruction,

> It was by faith that Joseph, when he was about to die, said confidently that the people of Israel would leave Egypt. He even commanded them to take his bones with them when they left. (Heb. 11:22, NLT)

The instruction of Joseph to the Israelites at that time was not a mere commandment but a covenant. This was carried out at the time of Moses.

> Moses took the bones of Joseph with him because Joseph had made the sons of Israel swear an oath. He had said, "God will surely come to your aid, and then you must carry my bones up with you from this place." (Exod. 13:19, NIV)

The covenant aspect of this deal really amplifies the importance of taking his bones. This definitely means that there is more to this "bones" thing.

What was taken out of Egypt were not just ordinary bones but a system of wealth building and sustenance. Since the bones were taken out, Egypt lost its status of a superpower, but despite it all, you can still see the remnants of this wealth building in Egypt due to a process called leaching or seepage. By virtue of the fact that the bones stayed in Egypt for 430 years, some residue of the bone or wealth-building system is still present and working for Egypt till today.

Despite the smallness of Israel numerically and in acreage, the wisdom and wealth of her citizens is beyond comprehension. This is because the bones of Joseph returned to the nation:

> Joseph's bones, which the People of Israel had brought from Egypt, they buried in Shechem in the plot of ground that Jacob had purchased from the sons of Hamor (who was the father of Shechem). He paid a hundred silver coins for it. It belongs to the inheritance of the family of Joseph. (Josh. 24:32, MSG)

When you take his bones with you, you are also taking a system of wealth creation and sustenance with you.

The word *bone* **symbolizes Structure**:

> And the bones of Saul and Jonathan his son they buried in the country of Benjamin in Zelah in the tomb of Kish, [Saul's] father, and they did all that the king commanded. And after that, God heard and answered when His people prayed for the land. (2 Sam. 21:14, TAB)

A structure is the mode of building, organizing, arranging, or constructing things. In chemistry, it is the manner in which atoms in a molecule are joined to each other, especially in organic chemistry, where molecular arrangement is represented by a diagram or model. In government, this is the art of governance or rulership.

There was a period of sadness in the life of one of the great prophets of Israel at that time –Samuel. This was when he perceived the people of Israel had rejected him because they wanted a king. He thought they were copying other nations, but he did not know that this also fit the plan of God for mankind. Everything was working together for good. His surprise was unquantifiable when God told him to allow them to have a king.

Before now they had judges. While one of the duties of the judges at that time was to act as an administrative head, they were mostly settling disputes. It was always quarrels, murmurings, and disagreements. God already had enough of that in the wilderness from the time of the first judge—Moses. Jehovah Rohi (Our Shepherd) knew that was not His plan for his people. His desire for them was to be royalty—kings. God is not a King of judges but The King of kings. The idea was for a king to have a kingdom to govern.

At that time, things were not right because He was not what He wanted to be. He had to move things to the way they ought to be. He himself selected the first king of Israel.

> Now the day before Saul came, the LORD had revealed this to Samuel: "About this time tomorrow I will send you a man from the land of Benjamin. Anoint him leader over my people Israel; he will deliver my people from the hand of the Philistines. I have looked upon my people, for their cry has reached me." When Samuel caught sight of Saul, the LORD said to him, "This is the man I spoke to you about; *he will govern my people.*" (1 Sam. 9:15–17, NIV)

What was released into the life of the Israelites through Saul was not simply a king but a structure of government or governmental authority. The know-how to rule, decree, authorize, subdue, dominate, and mandate was birthed (1 Sam. 8:11–18).

The Components

Even though Saul's bones were originally buried (1 Sam. 31:13), it had to be exhumed and buried properly in the tomb of Kish. It was after this that good government continued in the land of Israel (2 Sam. 21:14).

From the foregoing, we can see that bones mean **strength, safety, sameness, system,** and **structure**. All these attributes are present in both the divine and demonic kingdom. Satan also understands this; that is why you see various systems and structures in the world. The world will tell you that to get by you have to steal, bribe, lie, backbite, sell drugs, fornicate, prostitute, and engage in all manner of heinous crime.

Jehovah Adonai (the Sovereign God) knew all these, and he responded prophetically as a symbol of things to come during the Passover:

> In one house shall it be eaten [by one company]; you shall not carry any of the flesh outside the house; neither shall you break a bone of it. (Exod. 12:46, TAB)

This was during the consumption of the physical Passover lamb. But the real Passover lamb came in the flesh, and there was a day when there was war between the kingdom of darkness and light. To the natural eyes, darkness was going to consume light. The ratio was at least 2 to 1 in favor of darkness. Not only that, light was between darkness.

> It was the day of preparation, and the Jewish leaders didn't want the bodies hanging there the next day, which was the Sabbath (and a very special Sabbath, because it was the Passover). So they asked Pilate to hasten their deaths by ordering that their legs be broken. Then their bodies could be taken down. So the soldiers came and broke the legs of the two men crucified with Jesus. (John 19:31–32, NLT)

The two thieves crucified with Jesus symbolize a demonic kingdom. With the breaking of their bones, the competition between you and your progress has been broken. Every system of darkness and wealth stealing against you has been broken.

> God brought [Israel] forth out of Egypt; [Israel] has strength like the wild ox; he shall eat up the nations, his enemies,

crushing their bones and piercing them through with his arrows. (Num. 24:8, TAB)

As a child of God and a member of the commonwealth of Israel, you are out of Egypt, you have strength. It is time for you to eat up your enemies and crush their bones. Every system of failure, lack, and sin is an enemy, and I decree into your life that they are crushed today in Jesus's name, amen.

The Bible says, "But when they came to Jesus, they saw that he was already dead, so they didn't break his legs" (John 19:33, TAB).

Once again, let me take you back to what bones mean: they are *strength, safety, sameness, system,* and *structure.*

This means His strength, safety, sameness, system, and structure were not broken. Since these were not broken, it then means His strength is available for you.

What is in him (sameness) is also in you. They could not break it. It remains pure and undiluted.

As a child of God, there is a safety in Him for you. The name of the Lord is a strong tower the righteous run into it, and they are saved.

The system of excellence and wealth that he has is also available for you.

Though Jesus came from a humble background (he was not even born in a hospital), he never lacked. Anytime there was a need, there was always divine provision. As from today, you will never lack. As Jesus worked the system and it worked for Him, so shall it work for you.

The structure is the way of authority or governance. The Bible says concerning Jesus that the government shall be upon his shoulder and of the increase of His kingdom there shall be no end. From now on, whatever you ask to go shall go and whatever you ask to come shall come. Henceforth, you will not be like a bone out of joint.

> For the LORD protects the bones of the righteous; not one of them is broken! (Ps. 34:20, NLT)

I speak into your destiny that God will protect your bones from now on as you walk and work in His light.

Every one of your bones that is buried shall begin to arise and shine in Jesus's name. It is time for you to start speaking to your bones.

Pray the following:

1. Decree that every bone in your life will receive health in Jesus name. "Pleasant words are as an honeycomb, sweet to the soul, and health to the bones" (Prov. 16:24, KJV).

2. Ask God to restore every weak and broken bone in your life. "Make me to hear joy and gladness and be satisfied; let the bones which You have broken rejoice" (Ps. 51:8, TAB).

6

The Know How

> For we are members of his body, of his flesh, and of his bones. (Eph. 5:30, KJV)

While it is critical to know the meaning of *bones*, it is exceedingly crucial to know how you can take His bones with you. You need to know how to take His strength with you in the moment of weakness, how He can be your security in times of danger, how to respond to Satan when he sows the seed of doubt in your life as to who you are, and how to work His system and build His structure.

When the church is described, it is often compared to a body. The church is not a building but of human beings who have accepted Jesus Christ as their Lord and Savior. So, as an individual who has the license to succeed, you are likened to a body. The bone is part of the body. Therefore, before you can know how to carry His bones with you, you need to know how the bone is formed.

Once again, remember the five things that the bones represent: strength, security, sameness, systems, and structure.

In the study of embryology, we find out we begin as a cell. Two haploid cells (sperm and egg) fuse during fertilization to form a diploid cell called a zygote. After the formation of the zygote, there is then cleavage, and the diploid cells begin to divide again into multiple cells.

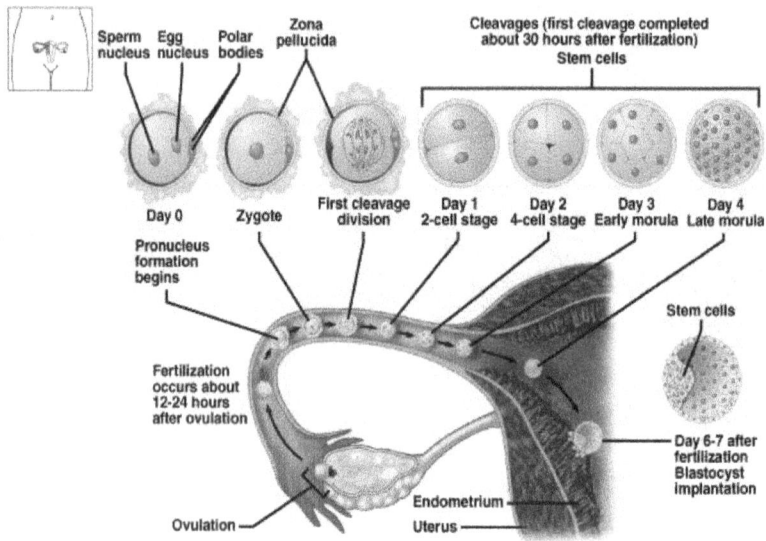

It is interesting to know that growth or formation of the body does not come with a mass swelling or increase but through a process of multiplication by division. If the zygote begins to grow or increase exponentially, it becomes a cancer. By the first day, you see what is called a first cleavage; by the second day, you also see another cleavage. This then leads to early and then late morula (the spherical embryonic mass of cells formed as a result of cleavage of the fertilized ovum).

This division is not a haphazard division, but one done with wisdom. *When you look at the different stages of growth from a zygote to a fully formed baby, you see a (you can take a guess) division into three main stages: first, second, and third trimesters. This aptly sums up the statement "Let us make man in our own image after our likeness." This is the involvement of the Trinity—God the Father, Son, and Holy Spirit—in creation hereby exemplified scientifically.* As the division is going on, there is formation of systems, sameness, safety, strength, and structure.

Sameness: this is how a baby can be born and the baby will look like either of the parents.

Safety or security: the baby is born with an immune system, which is further developed as the baby grows.

Structure: the ability to be tall or short is also present in the genes.

Strength: I need to explain this with my second child. I remember when she came out, she came out fighting. One of the nurses said, "This is a feisty one, hey!" Till today, she has strong willpower.

System: alimentary, nervous, etc., are also present.

The question that comes to our mind is, how does this relate to carrying the sameness, safety, strength, system, and structure with us wherever we go?

Simply put, through multiplication by division. This implies breaking down any problem, difficulty, or challenge into small components without losing the "bones"—sameness, safety, structure, strength, and system—to arrive at a solution.

It is the same concept knowledgeable individuals and established organizations employ. By the time organizations grow in net worth or client base, instead of allowing the same employees to carry the weight of the company, they divide the workload of the employees by adding staff without losing the integrity or value or vision of the company.

A principle to solving a problem is to divide it. When you break it down into smaller components, you are able to better grasp how to handle it. When a problematic situation occurs, a trick that the devil plays on us is to magnify the problem and make it larger than life. In some cases, we are unable to sleep. We toss and turn on our beds.

Remember what Jesus did when there was a storm. He was busy sleeping and, if I may add, snoring. The more turbulent or boisterous the storm, the more he snored—*zzzz*. I am sure the noise must have been very annoying to Satan and his demonic angels. Since they could not strike fear into the heart of Jesus, they succeeded in making his disciples panic.

When Jesus woke up, all He did was command the storm to be still. You must never allow Satan, difficulties, or challenges compromise the integrity of your "bones" by any form of degradation. Learn to use the concept of BODMAS or PEMDAS.

The Concept of BODMAS or PEMDAS

This is a principle used in mathematics to solve a problem. It simply means you need to break the problem into smaller units so that you can get an accurate answer. Remember, everything that God created answers to a system.

There is a story in the Bible that showed how a man who had the license to succeed carried His "bones" to fulfill his destiny. This will be a great story to use in explaining the concept of BODMAS or PEMDAS. Prior to this time, this individual had been bedeviled with the abnormal struggle syndrome. It was always endless labor. On a particular day, he was faced with the prospect of his destiny being terminated due to a previous "atrocity" he committed. The one he "swindled" had been patiently waiting for him.

Based on using the concept of BODMAS or PEMDAS, he followed a systematic order of operations to simplify the problem so that it became easily solvable.

Here is the story of the man called Jacob the son of Isaac and the grandson of Abraham:

> That night Jacob got up and took his two wives, his two maidservants and his eleven sons and crossed the ford of the Jabbok. After he had sent them across the stream, he sent over all his possessions. So Jacob was left alone, and a man wrestled with him till daybreak. When the man saw that he could not overpower him, he touched the socket of Jacob's hip so that his hip was wrenched as he wrestled with the man. Then the man said, "Let me go, for it is daybreak." But Jacob replied, "I will not let you go unless you bless me." The man asked him, "What is your name?" "Jacob," he answered. Then the man said, "Your name will no longer be Jacob, but Israel, because you have struggled with God and with men and have overcome." Jacob said, "Please tell me your name." But he replied, "Why do you ask my name?" Then he blessed him there. So Jacob called the place Peniel, saying, "It is because I saw God face to face, and yet my life was spared." The sun rose above him as he passed Peniel, and he was limping because of his hip. (Gen. 32:22–31, NIV)

The Know How

As the sun rose above Jacob (Israel), so shall the Sun of Righteousness with healing in His wings rise above you in Jesus's name, amen. For your sun to rise, some key principles, as exemplified by Jacob in the above story, need to be practiced. These principles are the building blocks for solving an arithmetic problem:

B—Brackets (bracket or group blessings)

O—Order (order your ways)

D—Division (divide distractions)

M—Multiplication (multiply wisdom)

A—Addition (add value)

S—Subtraction (subtract sin)

Some people are used to the version called PEMDAS, or "Please excuse my dear aunt Sally." It is mainly the same concept. The only difference is that Multiplication and Division are interchangeable:

P—Parentheses (bracket or group blessings)

E—Exponent (order your ways)

M—Multiplication (multiply wisdom)

D—Division (divide distractions)

A—Addition (add value)

S—Subtraction (subtract sin)

Bracket

Bracket is to encompass, group, or surround.

> Then the man said, "Let me go, for it is daybreak." But Jacob replied, "I will not let you go unless you bless me." (Genesis 32: 26, NIV)

Most times, the season of problems is always a season of promotion. The time of trials is always an opportunity to triumph, and the challenges you face will turn you to a champion. Jacob evaluated and sized up the situation and determined to do something about it. He identified that he was in the presence of the "blesser", and he refused to let him go because he wanted to be blessed.

> For [even the whole] creation (all nature) waits expectantly and longs earnestly for God's sons to be made known [waits for the revealing, the disclosing of their sonship]. (Rom. 8:19, TAB)

It's natural there is a law of gravity, but there is also a law of aerodynamics. When the law of aerodynamics collides with that of gravity, the law of gravity bows. The difference between people who go with the flow and those who are outstanding is while one decides "God's time is the best," the other decides to "create God's best time."

> The created world itself can hardly wait for what's coming next. (Rom. 8:19, MSG)

Esther, an orphan and a refugee, bracketed blessing. She approached the king when it wasn't the time to do so. Your approach to any situation will always determine your achievement. Esther was able to face the king—her husband—at a time when she was not supposed to venture into his presence because she carried the "bones" (strength, sameness, safety, system, and structure) with her.

She did not go into the presence of the king haphazardly. She prepared, fasted, bathed, dressed well, wore nice perfume, etc.

A season of performance requires a season of preparation.

It is always important you evaluate the situation you are in so that you can appropriately deal with it. Remember that every organ in your body started from a cell and, by continuous division, the organs were formed. Break down those challenges into small component parts so that you can bracket blessing. The license in you to succeed must be utilized.

Order

Order refers to a condition of methodical or prescribed arrangement among component parts such that proper functioning or appearance is achieved.

No matter the situation that you encounter, to effectively deal with it, you must be organized.

> That night Jacob got up and took his two wives, his two maidservants and his eleven sons and crossed the ford of the Jabbok. (Gen. 32: 22-23, NIV)

Though you may want to bracket blessing, there is still an immense need for order. When Jacob got to the brook, he did not just jump into the water, he identified the best point to cross the river. He was organized. He crossed the river at the ford, which is a shallow place in a body of water, such as a river, where one can cross by walking or riding on an animal or in a vehicle.

> Take a lesson from the ants, you lazybones. Learn from their ways and be wise! (Prov. 6:6, NLT)

Be organized, even in the face of adversity. The story below is about the way Nehemiah organized the Israelites when they were building the wall. It is a story that every man needs to study. He did not give room to the rumors and intimidation of the enemy. Instead, he organized himself and the workers to order their steps. After organizing them strategically, he encouraged them. Even when things started taking shape, he did not rest on his oars. He was still alert.

Please read on:

> The Jews who lived near the enemy came and told us again and again, "They will come from all directions and attack us!" So I placed armed guards behind the lowest parts of the wall in the exposed areas. I stationed the people to stand guard by families, armed with swords, spears, and bows. Then as I looked over the situation, I called together the leaders and the people and said to them, "Don't be afraid of the enemy! Remember the Lord, who is great and glorious, and fight for your friends, your families, and your homes!"

When our enemies heard that we knew of their plans and that God had frustrated them, we all returned to our work on the wall. But from then on, only half my men worked while the other half stood guard with spears, shields, bows, and coats of mail. The officers stationed themselves behind the people of Judah who were building the wall. The common laborers carried on their work with one hand supporting their load and one hand holding a weapon. All the builders had a sword belted to their side. The trumpeter stayed with me to sound the alarm.

Then I explained to the nobles and officials and all the people, "The work is very spread out, and we are widely separated from each other along the wall. When you hear the blast of the trumpet, rush to wherever it is sounding. Then our God will fight for us!" We worked early and late, from sunrise to sunset. And half the men were always on guard. I also told everyone living outside the walls to move into Jerusalem. That way they and their servants could go on guard duty at night as well as work during the day. During this time, none of us—not I, nor my relatives, nor my servants, nor the guards who were with me—ever took off our clothes. We carried our weapons with us at all times, even when we went for water. (Neh. 4:12–23, NLT)

Division

Division refers to the proportional distribution of a quantity or entity.

After he had sent them across the stream, he sent over all his possessions. So Jacob was left alone. (Gen. 32: 24, NIV)

Divide distraction. It is an entity. An entity is something that exists as a particular and discrete unit. You can sever the cord of distraction from yourself. Jacob separated himself from every form of distraction. After he "ordered" his wives and children by way of methodical arrangement, his possessions were sent packing to prevent any form of distraction. He was left alone. Distractions will derail you on your path to your destination (destiny).

> What I always feared has happened to me. What I dreaded has come to be. (Job 3:25, NLT)

Multiplication

> Then the man said, "Let me go, for it is daybreak." But Jacob replied, "I will not let you go unless you bless me." (Gen. 32: 26, NIV)

You need to multiply wisdom. At this point in the life of Jacob, he would have been tired, weary, sore, and in serious pain. Verse 25 begins with "When the man saw that he could not overcome Jacob." The challenge you have been going through cannot overcome you. The license to succeed is in you. Satan already knows he cannot overcome you.

Do you know that you could be winning while you think you are losing?

> *Learn to be wise*, and develop good judgment. (Prov. 4:5, NLT)

> Common sense in an uncommon degree is what the world calls wisdom. (Coleridge)

Jacob said you are not going anywhere. He wanted all that should be his despite his tired and tattered state. One important thing to note at this time is that Jacob had been previously blessed not only by his father, Isaac, but also by the Almighty God. He could have said, "I already have enough blessing," but he desired more—he wanted a multiplication of blessings.

Addition

Addition means to combine or to join with the aim of increasing; to augment.

> Then the man said, "Your name will no longer be Jacob, but Israel, because you have struggled with God and with men and have overcome." (Gen. 32: 28, NIV)

You need to add value to yourself. Jacob means "supplanter," but his name was changed to Israel, which means "princely strength." The land he was standing on became Peniel, meaning the "face of God." While crude oil has value, its worth is revealed after going to the refinery. It goes into the refinery singularly rough but comes out multiple refined. From the crude oil, you have gas-propane, petrol, kerosene, diesel, etc.

Subtraction

Subtraction means to take away or deduct.

> The man asked him, "What is your name?" "Jacob," he answered. (Gen. 32:27, NIV)

Take away sin. Jacob was asked, "What is your name?" He said, "Jacob," which simply describes him as a supplanter.

> For though your hearts were once full of darkness, now you are full of light from the Lord, and your behavior should show it! For this light within you produces only what is good and right and true. Try to find out what is pleasing to the Lord. Take no part in the worthless deeds of evil and darkness; instead, rebuke and expose them. (Eph. 5:8–11, NLT)

> And have no fellowship with the unfruitful works of darkness, but rather reprove them. (Eph. 5:11, KJV)

For you to be able to take the bones with you and not lose your license to succeed, you have to be dead to the lusts of the world but be alive in Him.

> But when they came to Jesus, they saw that he was already dead, so they didn't break his legs. (John 19:33, TAB)

The bones of Jesus were not broken, because he was already dead. He was therefore left alone. To effectively carry His bones with you, you have to be dead to the systems of the world that will try to tell you that success is only available to a few based on their earthly pedigree or lineage.

It is time for you to know who you are in Him and begin to work His principles and mysteries. Take time to evaluate the situation. Don't swallow the enemy's bait.

7

Don't Squint

> Your eyes are windows into your body. If you open your eyes wide in wonder and belief, your body fills up with light. If you live squinty-eyed in greed and distrust, your body is a dank cellar. If you pull the blinds on your windows, what a dark life you will have! (Matt. 6:22–23, MSG)

You must use "your windows" wisely in life. Always ensure that you can see clearly through the mirror of the Word.

Though the eyes are used descriptively in this passage as a window, the message that this is meant to convey is not the ornamental or positional representation of a window but its functionality.

In the Bible, you see certain things being used to describe some other things. For example, the Word of God is likened to a lamp (Ps. 119:115), hammer (Jer. 23:28–29), fire (Jer. 23:28–29), rock of offense (Rom. 9:33), and a two-edged sword (Heb. 4:12).

The eye is an organ of vision or light sensitivity. The word *eye* is used figuratively in the following expressions:

1. An "evil eye" to demonstrate envy or jealousy. "Am I not permitted to do what I choose with what is mine? [Or do you begrudge my being generous?] Is your eye evil because I am good?" (Matt. 20:15, TAB).

2. A "bountiful eye" to demonstrate generosity or benevolence. "He who has a bountiful eye shall be blessed, for he gives of his bread to the poor" (Prov. 22:9, TAB).

3. The term "haughty eyes" is used to demonstrate pride or arrogance. "A proud look [the spirit that makes one overestimate himself and underestimate others]" (Prov. 6:17, TAB).

4. The term "wanton eyes" is used to demonstrate undisciplined or flirtatious looks. "Because the daughters of Zion are haughty, And walk with outstretched necks and wanton eyes, Walking and mincing as they go, making a jingling with their feet" (Isa. 3:16, NKJV).

5. The term "adulterous eyes" to demonstrate seduction, harlotry, and covetousness. "They have eyes full of harlotry, insatiable for sin. They beguile and bait and lure away unstable souls. Their hearts are trained in covetousness (lust, greed), [they are] children of a curse [exposed to cursing]!" (2 Pet. 2:14, TAB).

6. The term "lustful eyes" is used to demonstrate want and greedy longings. "Practically everything that goes on in the world—wanting your own way, wanting everything for yourself, wanting to appear important—has nothing to do with the Father. It just isolates you from him. The world and all its wanting, wanting, wanting is on the way out—but whoever does what God wants is set for eternity." (1 John 2:16, MSG)

7. The term "eye-service" demonstrates doing things for show, or when an earthly superior can see you. "Not in the way of eye-service [as if they were watching you] and only to please men, but as servants (slaves) of Christ, doing the will of God heartily and with your whole soul" (Eph. 6:6, TAB).

In any gathering, group, organization, meeting, even in the church, these seven sets of eyes are present. This is an important reason why you have to wisely use the eyes you now have based on the conferment of the license to succeed upon you. Based on what you have been learning from this book thus far, you would have been seeing things in a different light. Therefore, use the windows wisely.

Don't Squint

The King James translation that says, "The light of the body is the eye: if therefore thine eye be single, thy whole body shall be full of light" (Matt. 6:22, KJV) clearly proclaims a condition that is necessary for the whole body to be full of light—a single eye.

When you look at God's creation and you observe that all living beings were created to have two eyes, the statement "Thine eye be single" appears to be a contradiction. Anybody with a single eye socket could be viewed as being disabled or a monster, but the singleness being advocated by Jesus has nothing to do with the physical number of eyes but what the eyes perceive.

The aim of Jesus in making this statement is to take a person or a people from where they were or are to where they should be. What the eyes see or perceive is based on the message translated to the eyes from the mind. Though we have heard of the term *color blindness*, it is what the mind wants the eyes to see that the eyes will see. The state of the eyes is dependent on the amount of light available to the eyes. While without light the eyes will not be able to function properly, with too much light, they can also be blind.

In the latter part of the verse, you see the effect of singleness. There is an exponential increase in its effect. While an organ of the body (the eyes) is expected to be "single" in its function, perception, and action, the whole body receives the benefit (thy whole body shall be full of light) of the singular action.

Everybody reading this has "at least" a pair of eyes. Notice the use of the phrase *at least*. At least because some have contact lenses and others have other forms of prescription lenses. One thing that everybody with eyes knows is that for you to be able to go in a specific direction, the eyes must work together to guide the limbs. Eye A cannot say, "I want to go backward," while eye B wants to go forward.

When an obstacle is seen, the proper message is relayed to the limbs through the brain so that the consequent danger of crashing into the obstacle is averted.

The same concept applies to a family, people, or organization. While we individually have eyes, for the body to have light, the eyes must be single (i.e., in agreement or have the same focus).

A man of God's testimony aptly describes this. At a time, God asked him how many eyes he has, to which he replied, "Two."

God furthermore said, "Can you make one to look up and the other look down at the same time?"

His response was, "No."

God then said, "Anytime you are looking at man, do not claim to be looking at me."

It is only those who look unto God who will not be ashamed.

In your family, business, and studies, there must be singularity of focus. Be in agreement with what the Word of God says you must do and be all that the Word of God says you must be.

One of the reasons why some eyes have lenses or an artificial aid on them is to assist in proper functioning and, in some cases, for aesthetics. Some of the eye problems people experience are also evident in everyday human endeavor:

- *Astigmatism.* A visual defect in which the unequal curvature of one or more refractive surfaces of the eye, usually the cornea, prevents light rays from focusing clearly at one point on the retina, resulting in blurred vision and imperfect image. Look at this:

  > Oh foolish Galatians! What magician has cast an evil spell on you? For you used to see the meaning of Jesus Christ's death as clearly as though I had shown you a signboard with a picture of Christ dying on the cross. (Galatians 3:1, NLT)

Some used to see clearly before astigmatism set in—backsliding. They were properly focused on fulfilling their purpose and destiny in life based on the Word of God, but now they do what they like. They have abolished the basic foundation of the faith and principles of God that is guaranteed to bring them progress. Anybody who continues in this direction of "astigmatism" is sure to lose the license to succeed.

A major reason why you will find yourself in such a mess is if you neglect the kingdom system for the world or old system. "Rather I make myself guilty if I rebuild the old system I already tore down" (Galatians 2:18, NLT).

Due to the fact that you experienced challenges or a curve in the road while utilizing your license to succeed does not mean you have to stop driving on the highway of life. This must not be so. You do not stop driving because the traffic is heavy. You either wait or take a legal detour to arrive at your destination.

To take away blurred vision, you cannot depend solely upon mere human intellect or worldly logic.

> What actually took place is this: I tried keeping rules and working my head off to please God, and it didn't work. So I quit being a "law man" so that I could be God's man. Christ's life showed me how, and enabled me to do it. I identified myself completely with him. Indeed, I have been crucified with Christ. My ego is no longer central. It is no longer important that I appear righteous before you or have your good opinion, and I am no longer driven to impress God. Christ lives in me. The life you see me living is not "mine," but it is lived by faith in the Son of God, who loved me and gave himself for me. I am not going to go back on that. (Galatians 2:19–20, MSG)

Stop doing it by yourself. Rely on the One who gave you the license in the first place.

- *Hyperopia.* An abnormal condition of the eye in which vision is better for distant objects than for near objects. It results from the eyeball being too short from front to back, causing images to be focused behind the retina. Also called farsightedness.

This condition in our everyday life can aptly be called hypocrisy.

You see everything bad in others, but what you need to take care of in your life, you neglect.

> And why worry about a speck in your friend's eye when you have a log in your own? How can you think of saying to your friend, "Let me help you get rid of that speck in your eye," when you can't see past the log in your own eye? Hypocrite! First get rid of the log in your own eye; then you will see well enough to deal with the speck in your friend's eye. (Matthew 7:3–5, NLT)

- *Myopia.* A condition of the eye in which parallel rays are focused in front of the retina, objects being seen distinctly only when near to the eye; nearsightedness.

This condition in normal life is nothing short of lack of foresight or discernment, obtuseness, or narrow-mindedness. This can also be described as living for today or the moment, or when you refuse to plan for the future.

> How can I account for this generation? The people have been like spoiled children whining to their parents, 'We wanted to skip rope, and you were always too tired; we wanted to talk, but you were always too busy'. (Matthew 11:16–17, MSG)

It is akin to behaving like toddlers, and it is time to stop behaving like spoiled children, when you do not take responsibility for the state or condition of your license and all you do is blame others.

> When I was a child, I talked like a child, I thought like a child, I reasoned like a child; now that I have become a man, I am done with childish ways and have put them aside. (1 Corinthians 13:11, TAB)

It is time for you to put away childish things. Stop thinking and reasoning like a child. Work the kingdom principles.

The law of success in the kingdom is different from that of the world:

1. Giving leads to prosperity (Luke 6:38, Prov. 11:24–25)

2. Waiting leads to winning (Isaiah 40:28–31)

3. Strength is from the joy of the Lord (Neh. 8:10)

4. Prayer is the source of power in the kingdom (Matt. 17:21)

5. Sacrifice leads to reward (Matt. 19:29)

6. Sorrow leads to life (2 Cor. 7:10–11)

8

20/20

Life is lived in stages, experienced at levels but established in dimension. Every stage, level or dimension that you find yourself in is for the glory of the Lord to be manifested. Your situation might be gory, your story unspeakable and unprintable but I want to declare into your destiny that in this year the glory of the Lord will fill your life in Jesus name, Amen.

Glory is a state of high honor, a radiant light, a brilliant beauty, a state of rejoicing or simply the overwhelming presence of the Lord. As with all things in life, if you stay on a spot for too long you become stagnant. Man has a desire to make progress.

Every situation no matter how terrible is glory in existence and glory about to multiply. This tells me without any iota of doubt that you are glory in existence and glory about to multiply. You may look at your life and say wait a minute what is he talking about? How can my life in such a deplorable state be termed glory? Have you considered that you are alive?

> "There is hope for a tree when it is cut down. It will sprout again. Its shoots will not stop sprouting. If its roots grow old in the ground and its stump dies in the soil, merely a scent of water will make it sprout and grow branches like a plant."
> (Job 14:7-9, GWT)

All you need is a scent of water. This is why the Bible declares that, "[There is no exemption] but he who is joined to all the living has hope--for a living dog is better than a dead lion." (Ecclesiastes 9:4, TAB)

These two verses of the scriptures vividly capture the reason why you should not count yourself or anybody out no matter the mess because the messenger can bring a message.

> "I will look to the LORD. I will wait for God to save me. I will wait for my God to listen to me. Don't laugh at me, my enemies. Although I've fallen, I will get up. Although I sit in the dark, the LORD is my light." (Micah 7:7-8, GWT)

> IN THE beginning God (prepared, formed, fashioned, and) created the heavens and the earth. The earth was without form and an empty waste, and darkness was upon the face of the very great deep. The Spirit of God was moving (hovering, brooding) over the face of the waters." (Genesis 1:1-2, TAB)

Many Bible scholars have looked at these two Bible verses and wondered about the Almighty God because, how can God create what is formless? The amplified version of the Bible breaks down the word created into three— prepared, formed and fashioned the heavens and the earth. What this immediately tells me is that if God spent time in preparation, knowledge in forming and wisdom in fashioning the earth it could not really have been formless and void.

> "The Lord by skillful and godly Wisdom has founded the earth; by understanding He has established the heavens." (Proverbs 3:19, TAB)

The state of the earth then was just waiting for value to be added. If the Almighty can prepare, form and fashion something and to the physical eyes it appears formless and void then it means God is up to something. If it appeared formless now, it definitely means it will not be formless forever because the Almighty declares the end from the beginning. He already finished gloriously what He wanted to achieve.

As regards your life, God is up to something. What people see or what you even see about your life at this moment is based on your interpretation that hinges on your vision. This is why your beginning is not from shame to glory but from glory to glory.

Though you may not have it all together yet, there could be an imperfection somewhere, the bank account may not be as buoyant as you will expect, the wife or husband could still be absent, the children could still be in the incubator after years of marriage, but you are still an embodiment of glory not shame.

Your origin, your foundation, the one who you are built on is not shame. God did not create you to be shamefaced but to be glorified.

And we know that all things work together for good to them that love God, to them who are the called according to his purpose. For whom he did foreknow, he also did predestinate to be conformed to the image of his Son, that he might be the firstborn among many brethren. Moreover, whom he did predestinate, them he also called: and whom he called, them he also justified: and whom he justified, them he also glorified. What shall we then say to these things? If God be for us, who can be against us? (Romans 8:28-31, KJV)

It is popularly said that the times of a man's life irrespective of the tide can be summarized into three—morning, noon and night or youngster, middle age and old man. At every one of these stages, it should be from glory to glory. Do not concentrate on the difficulties.

When his glory shows up in your life, he takes you from smallness to greatness. Do not despair. Utilize the license that heaven has given to you. People may say whatever they want concerning your destiny but with a smile based on your foundation in the Almighty God, follow the example of Philip to Nathanael by saying, "Come and see." (John 1:46)

As you have stepped into the Way of Righteousness, You Have The License To Succeed!

Be Gloriously Blessed!

PRAISE FOR *LICENSED TO SUCCEED*

"Every human wants to experience success in life! This is an indispensable reading for anyone who wants to understand his or her own potential for achieving greatness and to live life above the norm. This is a profound authoritative work that spans the wisdom of the ages and yet breaks new ground in its approach and will possibly become a classic in this and the next generation.

The author's approach to this timely issue brings a fresh breath of air that captivates the heart, engages the mind and inspires the spirit of the reader."

Dr. Myles Munroe

"The desire to succeed has been with man from time immemorial. This cannot be coincidental; it must be because it is in the DNA of man, just as it is in our nature to crave for food. Fruitfulness is productivity—"Pro and Duct." Creating the duct for the flow of ideas, concepts, breakthroughs and abundance.

Pastor Tayo Ojajuni has adequately, competently and robustly shown this ageless truth as the reason why those who know it rule and those who don't struggle. This powerful book has tremendous content and would bring transformation to the readers cerebral and spiritual life."

Pastor Matthew Ashimolowo

"A timeless, barrier-breaking, prejudice-overcoming, tenet-tearing, and creed-crushing pronouncement that has worked in the favor of every man or woman no matter his or her leaning is the statement "Let us make man in our image after our likeness" (Gen. 1:26, KJV) It shows that the intention of divinity for humanity is victorious living and this is still true today. The Almighty God spoke those words into the life of humanity not yet formed due to the extent of his love. Why then is success ephemeral to a lot of people? Many have the temporary permit but not the lifetime license. The book Licensed to Succeed will show you how to get the license and keep it."

Pastor Tayo Robert-Ojajuni (PTRO)

ABOUT THE AUTHOR

Olutayo Robert-Ojajuni was a software engineer for years before going into fulltime ministry as a pastor. At a time when he was lost and confused as to the way forward in life, he had a divine inspiration where certain things about life were explained. That encounter gave him a license to succeed.

Olutayo Robert-Ojajuni has also authored the book *Pillars of Greatness—Isaac Principles*. He lives in Toronto, Ontario with his wife and children where he is active at The Redeemed Christian Church of God and has a passion for music, Bible reading, and prayer in his spare time.

Readers can connect with Olutayo Robert-Ojajuni at:

www.thekingscovenant.ca
www.thekingsoasis.ca
https://www.youtube.com/user/CovenantChapelR
https://twitter.com/thekingscov https://www.instagram.com/thekingscov
https://www.facebook.com/thekingscov

Printed in the USA
CPSIA information can be obtained
at www.ICGtesting.com
LVHW091539221024
794497LV00002B/295

9 781038 300973